HOUSE OF LORDS

Science and Technology Committee

7 Day Loan

1st Report of Session 2005-06

Ageing: Scientific Aspects

Volume I: Report

Ordered to be printed 5 July 2005 and published 21 July 2005

Published by the Authority of the House of Lords

London : The Stationery Office Limited
£19.00 (inc VAT in UK)

HL Paper 20-I

CONTENTS

NOTE:

The Report of the Committee is published in Volume I, HL Paper No 20-I.
The Evidence of the Committee is published in Volume II, HL Paper
No 20-II.

Reference in the text of the Report as follows:

(Q) refers to a question in oral evidence

(p) refers to a page of written evidence

Ageing: Scientific Aspects

CHAPTER 1: EXECUTIVE SUMMARY

1.1. In June 2004 we appointed a Sub-Committee to examine the Scientific Aspects of Ageing. The matters we particularly wished to address are set out in the Call for Evidence we issued on 20 July 2004, which is set out in full in Appendix 3 to this report. We were especially interested in the biological processes of ageing, and in promising areas of research which might benefit older people and delay the onset of long-term illnesses and disabilities. We wished also to see how existing technologies, and research into new technologies, could be used to improve the quality of life of older people. In both of these fields we were anxious to see whether there was sufficient research capability in the United Kingdom, whether the correct research priorities had been identified, and how effectively research was coordinated.

1.2. The membership of the Sub-Committee is set out in Appendix 1. The Sub-Committee received 61 pieces of written evidence, and received oral evidence from 48 persons. A Seminar was held at the start of the inquiry.[1] In addition, members of the Sub-Committee visited the universities of Newcastle and York, and the Ellison Medical Foundation and the National Institute on Aging in Washington DC.[2]

1.3. A number of factors combined to make this an appropriate time for our inquiry: demographic changes, scientific progress, economic factors such as the cost of pensions and health care, rising expectations, and growing opportunities in an ageing world for exploiting the UK science base in ageing-related research.

1.4. The evidence we received from academic and other scientists showed that this is, as we suspected, an enormously exciting time for fundamental biological research into the causes of ageing, and into what can be done to slow the adverse effects of the ageing process and improve the quality of life of older people. In the case of the individual diseases which predominantly affect older people, research is also showing promising avenues of development in prevention and treatment.

1.5. It is of course always the case that such research would benefit from a greater input of funding, whether from the private sector, from charitable bodies or—crucially—from the public sector. However, quite apart from any shortage of funding, we found that research was being inhibited by two main factors which are the responsibility of the Government, and which they can and must take urgent steps to change. The first of these is the treatment of the scientific aspects of ageing as very much the junior partner in any consideration of older people. When the Government have appointed the Secretary of State for Work and Pensions as their "Champion of Older People", we regard it as disturbing that this Department chose not to submit written evidence to us. We comment on this more fully in Chapter 7.

---

[1] A full note of the Seminar is at Appendix 4.

[2] A full account of our visit is at Appendix 5.

1.6.   The second major factor inhibiting research is the extraordinary lack of coordination, in particular between the research councils. We chronicle in Chapter 8 the various different bodies which have been set up over time with the intention of providing such coordination, and how each has signally failed in this task. Advances can be made only if the coordination of research into ageing becomes an important responsibility of a major government department, headed by a minister responsible to Parliament for this.

1.7.   On the technology front the picture is different. Here, while new research could certainly lead to useful new developments, it is more the failure to apply existing technologies which we found disappointing. The technology is largely already there but, with few exceptions, it is not being applied nearly as much as it might to improve older people's quality of life. To some extent this is due to a lack of infrastructure, but largely it is the result of a failure of industry. This goes wider than the field of assistive technology: we have found a generalised failure by industry and commerce to recognise the enormous potential of the market which older people represent—a market which is already large, and which continues to grow. This is largely a matter for industry itself to resolve. A failure to do so will result in older people not benefiting from improvements to their quality of life which are there for the taking, but perhaps the chief sufferer will be UK industry itself.

1.8.   Maybe this is part of a wider problem. Old age is today still regarded in a very negative light. What concerns us is the pervasive but often unrecognised ageist attitude of the public and the media towards diseases prevalent in old age, and the ageist approach of industry to older people as consumers. We believe the Government could do more to help combat these attitudes, directly through government departments and the NHS, and indirectly by their influence on schools, industry and the media.

1.9.   Our aim in this report has been to make recommendations which may, first, help to increase the years of good health in old age, and secondly which may, if and when health does deteriorate, ensure that the quality of life is adversely affected as little as possible.

Structure of this report

1.10. We consider first the demographic changes which must form the background to any study of the problem. We then look at why and how ageing occurs. This leads to consideration of the ageing process, of the natural degeneration of the human body and mind over time, and of those diseases which are particularly prevalent in old age. Next we look at the environmental challenges, at assistive technology, and at the failure of industry to seize the opportunity to exploit a market which is there for the taking. We then consider management by the Government of health in old age, both for the individual and for society as a whole. After this we turn to the strategic direction and coordination of ageing-related research. We end with a summary of our conclusions and recommendations.

1.11. **Some of our conclusions and recommendations to the Government relate to matters which, in Scotland, Wales and Northern Ireland, are within the competence of the devolved administrations. To this extent, our recommendations are not directly addressed to those administrations; but insofar as many of the facts on which they are based do not respect administrative boundaries, we hope that the devolved administrations too will consider implementing our recommendations with any necessary amendments and modifications.**

Acknowledgements

1.12. We are grateful to all those who submitted written and oral evidence to the Sub-Committee, and to those who responded to their questions and submitted additional evidence. We are particularly grateful to the following persons and organisations:

- all those who took part in our seminar in September 2004, and the Academy of Medical Sciences, which hosted it;

- those who hosted our visits to the universities of Newcastle and York, and who provided evidence for us;

- in our visit to Washington DC, the staff of the British Embassy who arranged and facilitated our visit, the Ellison Medical Foundation, the National Institute on Aging, and all the members of their staff who made us welcome and gave us so generously of their time.

1.13. Throughout this inquiry we have been most fortunate to have as our specialist adviser Professor Thomas Kirkwood, Professor of Medicine and Co-Director of the Institute for Ageing and Health at the University of Newcastle-upon-Tyne. His expertise in the topic has been invaluable. We are most grateful to him for his enthusiasm, his help and his guidance. Professor Kirkwood has been careful to draw to our attention his potential conflicts of interest whenever these have arisen in the course of the inquiry. We stress that the conclusions we draw and recommendations we make are ours alone.

CHAPTER 2: BACKGROUND: DEMOGRAPHIC CHANGE

Introduction

2.1. Over the last two hundred years, life expectancy within industrialised nations such as the UK has doubled. More recently, life expectancy has also begun to increase across the developing world, and most nations are experiencing continuous upward trends in longevity. This astonishing feat—driven primarily by the successes of previous generations in combating early, preventable deaths—now evokes a curiously mixed response.

2.2. It is hardly possible to open a newspaper without reading of the increase in life expectancy, and the consequently rapidly increasing proportion of older people in the population. More often than not these matters are considered for the economic impact they will have, be it on the cost of healthcare or on pensions. The underlying tone of such discussion is often negative, focusing on the "burden" of increased numbers of older people and the threat of the demographic "timebomb".

2.3. These economic implications of changing life expectancy are without doubt of great importance, and have been the subject of a number of studies, not least by the House of Lords Select Committee on Economic Affairs.[3] However, when considering the future of ageing and its impacts upon society, it is important to understand what is actually happening to people from a biological and psychological perspective, since it is our bodies and minds—what happens to them and what we do with them—that are driving these changes. This inquiry has therefore considered these matters from the scientific perspective. We have looked at the biological processes of ageing, the application of research in technology and design to improve the quality of life of older people, and the funding and coordination of research in these areas.

2.4. The urgency of these matters is plain from the statistics. The 2001 Census showed that for the first time the number of people in England and Wales aged 60 and over was greater than the number aged under 16. The figures among the "oldest old" are even more striking. In 1951 there were 0.2 million people aged 85 and over; by 2001 this had grown to over 1.1 million.[4] Figures given at our seminar showed that the proportion of the global population aged 65 and over in 1900 was 1% (UK 5%); in 2000 it was 7% (UK 16%); and by 2050 it is estimated to be 20%, a figure the UK will probably reach in 2020.

2.5. Until very recently most observers and agencies concerned with forecasting future life expectancy predicted that it would soon reach a plateau, when the gains from preventing early death had been consolidated; the fixed, ineluctable reality of the ageing process would then be revealed. However, this has not happened. Life expectancy in the UK and other developed countries continues to increase by about two years per decade, so that for each hour spent in reading this report, life expectancy will have increased by 12 minutes. From studies in Sweden, where statistics have been kept since

---

[3] House of Lords Select Committee on Economic Affairs, 4th Report (2002-03): *Aspects of the Economics of an Ageing Population* (HL 179-I).

[4] Census 2001: First Results on Population for England and Wales, September 2002.

1860, it has been found that the increase in the year-by-year maximum life-span (age of the oldest person), far from slowing down towards a plateau, has been accelerating over the last 20 to 30 years.

2.6. No sensible work on ageing can be done without a detailed analysis of these demographic changes. We have considered the best available data, and have looked at UK data as compared with other countries. We have also looked at the very marked differences between social classes and between ethnic groups.

Life expectancy in the United Kingdom

2.7. The most reliable statistics on expectation of life in the UK are those collected and published by the Office for National Statistics (ONS). The figures take some time to collect and evaluate, and an inevitable consequence is that the statistics are based on figures going back a few years. There is however every reason to believe that the trends these figures demonstrate are continuing trends.

2.8. For males in the UK, life expectancy (LE) at birth has gone up from 70.8 in 1981 to 75.9 in 2002, an increase of 5.1 years; for females the figures are 76.8 and 80.5, an increase of 3.7 years. At age 70, LE for males has gone up from 10.1 to 12.6, for females from 13.3 to 15.2. However these figures mask considerable variations by geographical area. Male LE in 2002 was 76.2 in England, but in Scotland only 73.5. For females the figures are 80.7 and 78.9. Table 1 on page 12 shows life expectancy at different ages in each of the constituent parts of the UK between 1981 and 2002.[5]

2.9. These figures mask even more startling local variations. In 1996, in 16 local authority areas the LE was still below the average UK LE ten years earlier.[6] Within London, figures for male LE in 1998-2000 show that in Westminster this was 78.4, but just across the Thames in Lambeth it was only 73.5, while in Stratford, ten stops along the Jubilee line from Westminster, it was 72.7.[7] The figures for 2001-03, in table 2 on page 13, show that male LE in East Dorset was 80.1, eleven years longer than in Glasgow City (69.1). Figures for females show similar trends, but not quite so marked.[8]

5   Health Statistics Quarterly 25, Spring 2005, table 5.1.

6   Clare Griffiths and Justine Fitzpatrick, *Geographical Inequalities in Life Expectancy in the United Kingdom 1995-1997*, Health Statistics Quarterly 09, Spring 2001.

7   *Life Expectancy at Birth by Health and Local Authorities in the United Kingdom, 1998-2000*, Table 2, Health Statistics Quarterly 13, Spring 2002.

8   *Life Expectancy at Birth by Local Authorities in the United Kingdom, 1991-1993 and 2001-2003*, Health Statistics Quarterly 24, Winter 2004.

TABLE 1

Expectation of life at birth and selected age

Year	At birth (Males)	At age 5	20	30	50	60	70	80	Year	At birth (Females)	At age 5	20	30	50	60	70	80
United Kingdom																	
1981	70.8	66.9	52.3	42.7	24.1	16.3	10.1	5.8	1981	76.8	72.7	57.9	48.2	29.2	20.8	13.3	7.5
1986	71.9	67.8	53.2	43.6	24.9	16.8	10.5	6.0	1986	77.7	73.4	58.6	48.8	29.8	21.2	13.8	7.8
1991	73.2	68.9	54.2	44.7	26.0	17.7	11.1	6.4	1991	78.7	74.3	59.5	49.7	30.6	21.9	14.3	8.2
1996	74.3	69.8	55.1	45.6	26.9	18.5	11.6	6.6	1996	79.4	74.9	60.1	50.3	31.2	22.3	14.5	8.3
1997	74.5	70.1	55.4	45.9	27.2	18.8	11.7	6.7	1997	79.6	75.1	60.2	50.4	31.3	22.5	14.6	8.4
1998	74.8	70.3	55.6	46.1	27.4	18.9	11.9	6.7	1998	79.7	75.2	60.4	50.5	31.4	22.6	14.7	8.4
1999	75.0	70.6	55.9	46.3	27.6	19.2	12.0	6.8	1999	79.9	75.4	60.5	50.7	31.6	22.8	14.8	8.5
2000	75.4	70.9	56.2	46.6	28.0	19.5	12.3	7.0	2000	80.2	75.6	60.8	51.0	31.9	23.0	15.0	8.6
2001	75.7	71.2	56.5	46.9	28.3	19.8	12.5	7.1	2001	80.4	75.9	61.0	51.2	32.1	23.2	15.2	8.7
2002	75.9	71.5	56.7	47.2	28.5	20.0	12.6	7.2	2002	80.5	76.0	61.1	51.3	32.2	23.3	15.2	8.7
England and Wales																	
1981	71.0	67.1	52.5	42.9	24.3	16.4	10.1	5.8	1981	77.0	72.9	58.1	48.3	29.4	20.9	13.4	7.5
1986	72.1	68.0	53.4	43.8	25.0	16.9	10.5	6.1	1986	77.9	73.6	58.8	49.0	30.0	21.4	13.9	7.9
1991	73.4	69.1	54.4	44.8	26.1	17.8	11.2	6.4	1991	78.9	74.5	59.7	49.9	30.8	22.0	14.4	8.3
1996	74.5	70.1	55.4	45.8	27.1	18.7	11.6	6.6	1996	79.6	75.1	60.2	50.4	31.3	22.5	14.6	8.4
1997	74.8	70.3	55.6	46.1	27.4	18.9	11.8	6.7	1997	79.7	75.2	60.4	50.6	31.5	22.6	14.7	8.4
1998	75.0	70.6	55.8	46.3	27.6	19.1	11.9	6.8	1998	79.9	75.4	60.5	50.7	31.6	22.7	14.8	8.4
1999	75.3	70.8	56.1	46.5	27.8	19.3	12.1	6.9	1999	80.1	75.6	60.8	50.9	31.8	22.9	14.9	8.5
2000	75.6	71.2	56.4	46.9	28.1	19.6	12.3	7.0	2000	80.3	75.8	61.0	51.1	32.0	23.1	15.1	8.6
2001	76.0	71.5	56.7	47.2	28.5	19.9	12.6	7.1	2001	80.6	76.0	61.2	51.4	32.2	23.3	15.2	8.7
2002	76.2	71.7	57.0	47.4	28.7	20.1	12.7	7.2	2002	80.7	76.1	61.3	51.5	32.3	23.4	15.3	8.7
England																	
1981	71.1	67.1	52.5	42.9	24.3	16.4	10.1	5.8	1981	77.0	72.9	58.2	48.4	29.4	20.9	13.4	7.5
1986	72.2	68.1	53.4	43.8	25.1	17.0	10.6	6.1	1986	77.9	73.6	58.8	49.0	30.0	21.4	13.9	7.9
1991	73.4	69.1	54.4	44.9	26.2	17.8	11.2	6.4	1991	78.9	74.5	59.7	49.9	30.8	22.0	14.4	8.3
1996	74.5	70.1	55.4	45.9	27.1	18.7	11.7	6.6	1996	79.6	75.1	60.3	50.5	31.3	22.5	14.6	8.4
1997	74.8	70.4	55.6	46.1	27.4	18.9	11.8	6.7	1997	79.8	75.3	60.4	50.6	31.5	22.6	14.7	8.4
1998	75.0	70.6	55.9	46.3	27.6	19.1	12.0	6.8	1998	79.9	75.4	60.6	50.7	31.6	22.7	14.8	8.5
1999	75.3	70.9	56.1	46.6	27.9	19.4	12.1	6.9	1999	80.1	75.6	60.8	50.9	31.8	22.9	14.9	8.5
2000	75.7	71.2	56.5	46.9	28.2	19.6	12.4	7.0	2000	80.4	75.8	61.0	51.2	32.0	23.1	15.1	8.6
2001	76.0	71.5	56.8	47.2	28.5	19.9	12.6	7.1	2001	80.6	76.1	61.2	51.4	32.3	23.4	15.3	8.7
2002	76.2	71.8	57.0	47.4	28.7	20.1	12.8	7.2	2002	80.7	76.2	61.3	51.5	32.4	23.4	15.3	8.7
Wales																	
1981	70.4	66.5	51.9	42.2	23.6	15.8	9.7	5.6	1981	76.4	72.3	57.5	47.7	28.9	20.5	13.1	7.4
1986	71.6	67.5	52.8	43.2	24.6	16.6	10.3	6.0	1986	77.5	73.3	58.5	48.7	29.7	21.1	13.7	7.8
1991	73.1	68.8	54.1	44.6	25.8	17.6	11.0	6.4	1991	78.8	74.3	59.5	49.7	30.6	21.8	14.3	8.3
1996	73.9	69.4	54.7	45.3	26.6	18.2	11.3	6.4	1996	79.1	74.6	59.7	49.9	30.9	22.1	14.4	8.3
1997	74.3	69.8	55.1	45.6	26.9	18.5	11.6	6.6	1997	79.3	74.8	60.0	50.2	31.1	22.3	14.5	8.4
1998	74.4	70.0	55.2	45.8	27.1	18.6	11.6	6.6	1998	79.4	74.9	60.0	50.2	31.1	22.3	14.5	8.3
1999	74.7	70.2	55.5	46.1	27.4	18.9	11.9	6.8	1999	79.6	75.1	60.2	50.4	31.3	22.5	14.6	8.4
2000	74.9	70.5	55.8	46.3	27.6	19.1	12.0	6.8	2000	79.8	75.3	60.4	50.6	31.5	22.6	14.7	8.4
2001	75.4	70.9	56.2	46.7	28.0	19.5	12.3	7.1	2001	80.1	75.5	60.6	50.8	31.8	22.9	14.9	8.5
2002	75.7	71.1	56.3	46.9	28.2	19.7	12.4	7.1	2002	80.2	75.6	60.7	50.9	31.8	22.9	15.0	8.6
Scotland																	
1981	69.1	65.2	50.6	41.1	22.9	15.4	9.6	5.5	1981	75.3	71.2	56.4	46.7	27.9	19.7	12.7	7.2
1986	70.2	66.0	51.4	41.9	23.5	15.8	9.9	5.7	1986	76.2	71.9	57.1	47.3	28.4	20.1	13.0	7.5
1991	71.4	67.1	52.5	43.0	24.6	16.6	10.4	6.1	1991	77.1	72.7	57.9	48.1	29.2	20.7	13.5	7.9
1996	72.2	67.8	53.1	43.7	25.3	17.3	10.9	6.3	1996	77.9	73.3	58.5	48.7	29.8	21.2	13.8	8.0
1997	72.4	68.0	53.3	43.9	25.6	17.5	11.0	6.4	1997	78.0	73.5	58.7	48.9	30.0	21.4	13.9	8.0
1998	72.6	68.2	53.5	44.2	25.8	17.8	11.1	6.5	1998	78.2	73.6	58.8	49.0	30.1	21.4	13.9	8.0
1999	72.8	68.4	53.7	44.4	26.0	18.0	11.3	6.6	1999	78.4	73.8	59.0	49.2	30.3	21.6	14.0	8.1
2000	73.1	68.6	53.9	44.6	26.3	18.2	11.5	6.6	2000	78.6	74.0	59.2	49.4	30.5	21.8	14.1	8.1
2001	73.3	68.8	54.2	44.8	26.6	18.4	11.7	6.8	2001	78.8	74.2	59.4	49.6	30.7	22.0	14.3	8.2
2002	73.5	69.0	54.3	45.0	26.7	18.6	11.8	6.8	2002	78.9	74.3	59.5	49.7	30.8	22.1	14.4	8.2
Northern Ireland																	
1981	69.2	65.4	50.9	41.5	23.2	15.6	9.7	5.8	1981	75.5	71.6	56.8	47.1	28.3	20.0	12.8	7.3
1986	70.9	66.8	52.2	42.7	24.2	16.4	10.4	6.2	1986	77.1	72.9	58.1	48.3	29.3	20.8	13.4	7.8
1991	72.6	68.2	53.6	44.1	25.5	17.3	11.0	6.4	1991	78.4	74.0	59.2	49.4	30.3	21.6	14.2	8.3
1996	73.8	69.4	54.7	45.3	26.6	18.2	11.4	6.6	1996	79.2	74.7	59.9	50.0	30.9	22.1	14.4	8.4
1997	74.2	69.7	55.0	45.5	26.8	18.4	11.5	6.6	1997	79.5	75.0	60.2	50.3	31.2	22.4	14.5	8.4
1998	74.3	69.8	55.2	45.7	27.0	18.6	11.6	6.6	1998	79.5	75.0	60.2	50.4	31.2	22.4	14.5	8.2
1999	74.5	70.0	55.4	45.9	27.2	18.8	11.7	6.6	1999	79.6	75.1	60.2	50.4	31.3	22.5	14.6	8.2
2000	74.8	70.4	55.7	46.2	27.6	19.1	11.9	6.6	2000	79.8	75.2	60.4	50.6	31.5	22.6	14.6	8.2
2001	75.2	70.7	56.1	46.6	27.9	19.4	12.3	6.9	2001	80.1	75.6	60.7	50.9	31.8	22.9	14.9	8.4
2002	75.6	71.1	56.4	46.9	28.2	19.7	12.4	7.0	2002	80.4	75.9	61.0	51.2	32.0	23.1	15.1	8.5

Note:Figures from 1981 are calculated from the population estimates revised in the light of the 2001 Census. All Figures are based on a three-year period.

TABLE 2

Life Expectancy by Local Authority, 2001-03

Local authorities with the highest and lowest life expectancy at birth in the United Kingdom 2001-2003, and comparisons with 1991-1993

Males

Highest life expectancy		2001-2003	1991-1993	1991-1993
Rank	Local Authority	Years	Years	Rank
I	East Dorset	80.1	77.9	I
2	Hart	80.0	76.8	4
3	Kensington and Chelsea	79.8	73.0	301
4	Purbeck	79.7	75.6	47
5	South Cambridgeshire	79.4	76.0	24
6	Brentwood	79.4	74.8	127
7	South Norfolk	79.3	76.7	6
8	New Forest	79.3	75.8	29
9	Uttlesford	79.3	76.3	12
10	North Dorset	79.2	75.5	62
Lowest life expectancy				
432	Glasgow City	69.1	68.2	432
431	Inverclyde	70.2	69.6	429
430	West Dunbartonshire	70.8	69.5	431
429	Comhairle nan Eilean Siar	71.6	70.6	424
428	Manchester	71.8	69.6	430
427	Renfrewshire	71.9	70.5	427
426	North Lanarkshire	71.9	70.2	428
425	Dundee City	72.0	71.1	416
424	Blackpool	72.0	71.6	390
423	East Ayrshire	72.5	71.5	397

Local authorities with the highest and lowest life expectancy at birth in the United Kingdom 2001-2003, and comparisons with 1991-1993

Females

Highest life expectancy		2001-2003	1991-1993	1991-1993
Rank	Local Authority	Years	Years	Rank
I	Kensington and Chelsea	84.8	80.0	129
2	Epsom and Ewell	84.1	80.3	82
3	Guildford	83.9	81.6	7
4	Rutland	83.7	81.0	22
5	Christchurch	83.6	81.9	4
6	Hart	83.4	80.6	50
7	East Dorset	83.4	82.5	I
8	Alnwick	83.3	79.6	192
9	Cotswold	83.2	81.8	6
10	Mole Valley	83.2	81.0	23
Lowest life expectancy				
432	Glasgow City	76.4	75.0	432
431	North Lanarkshire	77.4	75.9	430
430	West Dunbartonshire	77.4	77.1	404
429	Blackburn with Darwen	77.6	77.0	406
428	Liverpool	77.7	77.0	407
427	West Lothian	77.7	77.0	408
426	Dundee City	77.8	76.8	416
425	Inverclyde	77.8	75.5	431
424	Manchester	77.8	76.4	427
423	Salford	77.9	76.5	425

Local authorities with the highest and lowest life expectancy at birth in the United Kingdom 1991-1993, and comparisons with 2001-2003

Males

Highest life expectancy		1991-1993	2001-2003	2001-2003
Rank	Local Authority	Years	Years	Rank
I	East Dorset	77.9	80.1	I
2	Mole Valley	77.1	78.3	50
3	Christchurch	76.9	78.2	58
4	Hart	76.8	80.0	2
5	Elmbridge	76.8	79.0	12
6	South Norfolk	76.7	79.3	7
7	Chelmsford	76.7	78.2	57
8	Wokingham	76.7	78.9	13
9	Waverley	76.7	78.5	39
10	Suffolk Coastal	76.6	78.3	54
Lowest life expectancy				
432	Glasgow City	68.2	69.1	432
431	West Dunbartonshire	69.5	70.8	430
430	Manchester	69.6	71.8	428
429	Inverclyde	69.6	70.2	431
428	North Lanarkshire	70.2	71.9	426
427	Renfrewshire	70.5	71.9	427
426	Tower Hamlets	70.6	72.9	419
425	Moyle	70.6	76.8	188
424	Comhairle nan Eilean Siar	70.6	71.6	429
423	Hammersmith and Fulham	70.8	75.8	270

Local authorities with the highest and lowest life expectancy at birth in the United Kingdom 1991-1993, and comparisons with 2001-2003

Females

Highest life expectancy		1991-1993	2001-2003	2001-2003
Rank	Local Authority	Years	Years	Rank
I	East Dorset	82.5	83.4	7
2	Stevenage	82.2	80.1	300
3	East Devon	82.0	82.8	28
4	Christchurch	81.9	83.6	5
5	Oadby and Wigston	81.8	81.5	140
6	Cotswold	81.8	83.2	9
7	Guildford	81.6	83.9	3
8	Chiltern	81.5	83.1	13
9	Waverley	81.5	82.2	57
10	Cambridge	81.4	81.7	106
Lowest life expectancy				
432	Glasgow City	75.0	76.4	432
431	Inverclyde	75.5	77.8	425
430	North Lanarkshire	75.9	77.4	431
429	Easington	75.9	78.3	416
428	Burnley	76.3	78.1	418
427	Manchester	76.4	77.8	424
426	Strabane	76.5	79.3	373
425	Salford	76.5	77.9	423
424	North Ayrshire	76.5	78.5	411
423	Corby	76.7	79.2	382

Inequalities between social classes

2.10. Social factors play a major part in these local divergences. The following criteria were used by the Registrar-General to define social class:[9]

BOX 1

Definition of Social Class

REGISTRAR GENERAL'S SOCIAL CLASS (BASED ON OCCUPATION)	
Class Description	**Examples of occupations**
Non-manual	
I Professional	Doctors, chartered accountants, professionally qualified engineers
II Managerial and technical/inter-mediate	Managers, school teachers, journalists
IIIN Skilled non-manual	Clerks, cashiers, retail staff
Manual	
IIIM Skilled manual	Supervisors of manual workers, plumbers, electricians, goods vehicle drivers
IV Partly skilled	Warehousemen, security guards, machine tool operators, care assistants, waiters and waitresses
V Unskilled	Labourers, cleaners and messengers

In 1996 the difference in LE between Social Classes I and V was 9.5 years for men and 6.4 years for women. The gap between the social classes is apparently narrowing; by 1999 it was down to 7.4 years for men and 3.1 years for women.[10] However care needs to be taken in interpreting underlying trends from short-term differences, when many factors may be at play. For instance, the reduction in the social-class gap LE for women between 1996 and 1999 was caused more by a decrease in the LE of women of Social Class I than by an increase in the LE of those in Social Class V.[11] The causes of these inequalities are many, complex, and interrelated; we consider some of them in the following chapter.[12]

---

[9]   These were the criteria used at the time of the study referred to. From 2001 they have been replaced by the National Statistics Socio-economic Classification.

[10]   Lin Hattersley, *Trends in Life Expectancy by Social Class – an update,* Health Statistics Quarterly 02, Summer 1999.

[11]   Angela Donkin, Peter Goldblatt and Kevin Lynch, *Inequalities in Life Expectancy by Social Class 1972-1999,* Health Statistics Quarterly 15, Autumn 2002.

[12]   Paragraph 3.

Differences between ethnic groups

2.11. The 2001 Census showed that only 14.5% of minority ethnic groups were aged 50+, compared to 35.1% of whites; while only 0.3% of minority ethnic groups were aged 85+, compared to 2.1% of whites. The full figures, in percentages of older people in each ethnic group, were:[13]

TABLE 3

Age Distribution by Ethnic Group, 2001

Aged :	50–64	65–84	85 +	All 50+
White	**18.2**	**14.9**	**2.1**	**35.1**
Mixed	4.7	2.7	0.3	7.6
All Asian or Asian British	**10.3**	**5.0**	**0.3**	**15.5**
Indian	12.8	6.2	0.3	19.4
Pakistani	7.4	3.9	0.2	11.5
Bangladeshi	6.4	3.1	0.1	9.6
All Black or Black British	**9.9**	**6.2**	**0.3**	**16.4**
Black Caribbean	13.4	10.2	0.4	24.0
Black African	6.8	2.2	0.1	9.1
Chinese	**11.1**	**4.8**	**0.3**	**16.2**
Other ethnic groups	11.0	2.7	0.2	13.9
All non-White minority ethnic population	**9.4**	**4.8**	**0.3**	**14.5**
All population	**17.5**	**14.0**	**1.9**	**33.5**

2.12. This is graphically illustrated by the following chart:[14]

FIGURE 1

Age Distribution by Ethnic Group, 2001-02

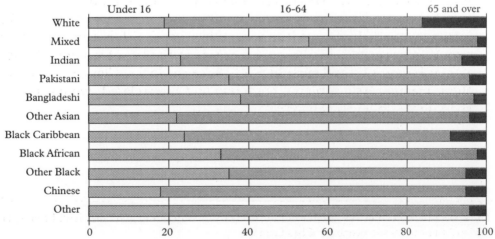

13 Office for National Statistics.

14 Office for National Statistics, *Focus on Older People 2004*, May 2004.

These distributions are to some extent the product of differences in LE, but also reflect the ages at which immigrants enter this country, and the length of time they have been here.

2.13. Ethnic minorities form a greater proportion of the lower social groups. It is a matter of fact that life expectancy is lower among ethnic minorities, but it is not clear to what extent this is due to the factors affecting all members of the lower social groups. The effect on ageing of distinctions attributable solely to ethnic differences is a matter we consider in Chapter 3.[15]

International comparisons

2.14. International comparisons are instructive. If the percentage of the population aged 65 and over is taken as a measure, of the 30 countries with the oldest populations, all but four are European. Japan is the only non-European country in the top 17. Italy tops the list with 18.8% of its population 65 and over; the UK is fourteenth with 15.7%. By comparison the United States is a young country, with only 12.4% aged 65 and over.[16]

2.15. A different but equally instructive measure of population ageing is provided by life expectancy at birth. The following figures[17] show LE, averaged for males and females, in the major countries of the European Union and a number of other selected nations:

Japan	81.5
Sweden	80.0
Canada	79.3
Spain	79.2
Australia	79.1
Switzerland	79.1
France	78.9
Norway	78.9
Belgium	78.7
Italy	78.7
Austria	78.5
Netherlands	78.3
Germany	78.2
Greece	78.2
New Zealand	78.2
United Kingdom	**78.1**
Finland	77.9
United States	77.0
Ireland	76.9
Cuba	76.7
Portugal	76.1
Poland	73.8
Hungary	71.7
Russian Federation	66.7

---

[15] Paragraphs 3.42 to 3.45.

[16] Older Americans 2004, Federal Interagency Forum on Aging-Related Statistics.

[17] UN World Population Prospects 1950-2050, 2002 revision.

The significance of these figures is that in the UK, despite its sustained high economic performance, and after half a century of a comprehensive National Health Service, LE still lags slightly behind the average for the high-income OECD States, which is 78.3.

2.16. **At current rates, life expectancy within the UK is increasing at the rate of about two years for each decade that passes. The consequences of this demographic change for all aspects of life are profound. As this Report will show, we have found little evidence that policy has been sufficiently informed by scientific understanding of the ageing process.**

Healthy Life Expectancy

2.17. We believe that increases in life expectancy are truly to be welcomed only if the "added years" are years of relative good health. We therefore also looked at figures which indicate to what extent healthy life expectancy (HLE) has kept pace with LE. We immediately came up against a problem of definition. As with all statistics relating to future projections, there is a margin of error in the figures for life expectancy. But while there is no possibility of error in determining when life begins and ends, good and bad health are far from being absolutes. They are often a matter of impression, and the line between the two is not a sharp one.

2.18. The ONS gave us the following information about methods of estimating HLE in the UK:

BOX 2

Methods of Estimating Healthy Life Expectancy

Healthy life expectancy is based on either **self-assessed** general health or **self-assessed** limiting long-standing illness. Whereas assessment of mortality is from vital registration, morbidity data are obtained using a subjective assessment by the individual.

Prevalence rates of ill-health for both these measures are derived from the British General Household Survey (GHS). This is a continuous nationally representative interview survey of residents in private households, including each year about 25,000 individuals of whom around 4,000 are aged 65 and over. The data used for HLE are based on a three-year moving average of rates reported for the central year so that they reflect the format of the life tables based on three years worth of mortality data produced by the Government Actuary's Department.

The GHS only includes residents in private households. However residents in communal establishments represent a significant proportion of the elderly and of those in ill-health. The HLE figures are adjusted to take into account the health of residents in health and care institutions. The ill-health rate for residents of communal establishments was estimated using the 1991 Census question on LLSI and applied to every year of the analysis. Population figures for residents in communal establishments were calculated using linear interpolation and extrapolation between the 1981 and 1991 populations.

SURVEY QUESTIONS USED TO CALCULATE ILL-HEALTH RATES

Limiting long-standing illness

GHS:

Do you have any long-standing illness, disability or infirmity? By long-standing I mean anything that has troubled you over a period of time or that is likely to affect you over a period of time. Yes/No

If "Yes":

(a) What is the matter with you?

(b) Does this illness or disability (do any of these illnesses or disabilities) limit your activities in any way? Yes/No

1991 CENSUS:

Do you have any long-term illness, health problem or handicap which limits your daily activities or the work you can do? Yes/No

General Health

GHS and 1991 CENSUS:

Over the last 12 months would you say your health has on the whole been good, fairly good, or not good?

2.19. Professor Sally Davies, the Director of Research and Development at the Department of Health, told us that figures obtained in this way, far from supporting the proposition that HLE is increasing at a faster rate than LE (as one might have hoped), or at least keeping pace with it, is in fact growing more slowly, so that there is a corresponding increase in what might be termed "unhealthy life expectancy" (Q 139). She subsequently drew our attention to the following graph, which strikingly illustrates this:

FIGURE 2

Life Expectancy and Healthy Life Expectancy

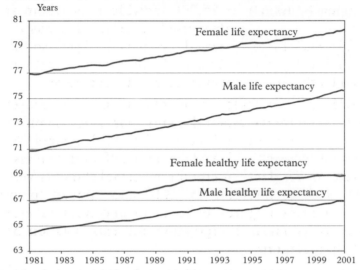

2.20. If this apparent increase in unhealthy life expectancy is a true reflection of the facts, it is a matter of considerable concern. We wondered however if this might simply be a reflection of the inaccuracy of self-assessment of so vague a concept as ill-health, and we asked the ONS whether this was a reliable method of calculation. They told us:

"A morbidity measure based on self-assessed health provides valuable information on the relevance of illness to the individual. A comparison of evidence by Ilder and Benyamini established that simple measures of self-rated health consistently predict subsequent morbidity, health care use and mortality, after controlling for risk factors and diagnosed conditions. While self-assessed health status is recognised as a valid measure of population health, concerns remain about the reliability of subjective assessments in general. These are known to vary systematically across population sub-groups (by ethnicity and social class) and over time. They reflect difference in ill-health, behaviour, expectations and cultural norms for health.

We know little about the sources of health perceptions, and what people are telling us when they report 'good', 'fairly good' or 'not good' health, or what is the underlying mechanism which consistently links perceived health status with other health-related outcomes. However self-perceived health has been repeatedly shown to be predictive of health outcomes. The most dramatic influence is seen in the association between self-rated health and subsequent mortality."

2.21. As an explanation of the apparent widening of the gap between LE and HLE, the ONS had this to say:

"There are several theories behind the increase in reported ill-health. It is possible to separate these ideas into the following six broad categories:

(1) People have become more sensitive about health or have adopted higher expectations about their health and/or functioning. The result is that conditions that would not earlier have been regarded as problems are now considered to impact on daily living. Any changes in morbidity over time may reflect people's expectations of good health as well as changes in incidence or duration.

(2) Economic incentives are persuading people more readily to consider or present themselves as ill. Workers are suspected of having target incomes, below which they are more inclined to work and it is suggested that rising real income has promoted more ill-health time, or higher incidence of injuries.

(3) Improvements in survey methods have led to the discovery of a growing proportion of health problems.

(4) Diseases, especially chronic diseases, are being detected earlier. The prevalence of those diseases has risen because the point at which sickness is said to have begun is now earlier. People examined or screened and found sick, the 'earlier patients', add to the prevalence of disease. In the case of diabetes, for example, earlier detection allows progress of the disease to be arrested and permits the sufferer to carry out ordinary activities despite to continued presence of the disease.

(5) People with ill-health are living longer. Illnesses and injuries that, in former times, were resolved in death are now more often resolved in management of the disease.

(6) The last century has seen a substitution in health risks. On the whole, illnesses with a short course and higher incidence, such as infectious diseases, have been replaced by diseases with a long course and low incidence, for example chronic conditions. This leads to an expansion in morbidity prevalence values, even when incidence remains the same over time.

Each hypothesis provides a plausible explanation for increase in the prevalence of ill-health. Untangling the differential trends in incidence, duration and prevalence of ill-health is only possible using longitudinal data. Many of the issues related to observed increases in ill-health rates in cross-sectional surveys will be addressed in the future using results from the English Longitudinal Study of Ageing."

2.22. These are all possible explanations for a *perceived* increase in "unhealthy life expectancy". However we have received no specific evidence showing whether the increase is wholly perceived, or a reflection of a true increase in years of ill-health in later life, or (as seems more likely) a combination of the two. In the case of a perceived increase, we do not know to what extent each of the reasons suggested by the ONS is actually responsible for the increase. If there is a true increase in ill-health, no explanation for this has been suggested to us.

2.23. It appears to us that questions based on self-assessment of such a vague concept as health, while they may enable comparisons to be made with replies to the same questions from different groups or different areas, are simply not sufficiently reliable to provide an effective objective measure of health in old age. Moreover, the questions asked often differ. While the GHS and 1991 Census asked for health to be classed as "good, fairly good, or not good", Department of Health (DoH) surveys have adopted criteria recommended in 1996 by the WHO, and have asked whether health is classed as "very good, good, fair, bad or very bad". Nor can international comparisons usefully be made, since other countries rely on yet other criteria. For example, the United States, Canada and Australia ask whether health is perceived as "excellent, very good, good, fair or poor"; in those countries, those who perceive their health to be "fair" are in the fourth category rather than the third.[18]

2.24. Ms Susan Lonsdale, Acting Head of the DoH Policy Research Programme, equated healthy life expectancy with disability-free life expectancy (Q 140), but other witnesses drew a clear distinction between the two. Sir John Grimley Evans, Emeritus Professor of Clinical Geratology at Oxford University, told us:

"Most geratologists have since [1984] focused on disability rather than morbidity as the crucial transition, because it is disability and its associated loss of autonomy that older people fear, and which in turn leads to dependency with its cost implications for the health and social services. Moreover, much of modern medicine as applied to older people does not 'cure' disease but relieves its symptoms and other effects and, in the best case, prolongs survival. People may still have the 'disease' in a medical sense but it does not affect their quality of life. Such effects ought surely to register as success in prolonging disability-free life expectancy, rather than as failure in extending the duration of (irrelevant) 'disease' … I would urge the Committee to focus on disability-free life expectancy rather than healthy life expectancy as a measure of the well-being of an ageing population."[19]

2.25. Sir John explained that it was generally accepted that the prevalence of disability in later life had fallen in the United States since the 1980s,[20] but that as far as the UK was concerned "the informed view is that we simply do not know what is happening, but there is certainly no evidence that disability levels in later life are falling as in the USA". Evidence that we received during our visit to the United States National Institute on Aging was to the same effect; Dr John Haaga, deputy associate director of the Behavioral and Social Research Program, suggested that in the United States, unlike the UK, HLE had been rising at the same rate as LE over previous years.[21]

2.26. In Sir John's view, what had happened in the United States could be made to happen here through appropriate health, social and educational policy. It was therefore highly desirable that disability free life expectancy in the general population should be monitored. This would not only assess the effectiveness of relevant government policy, but would also provide a more secure basis for recognising current shortfalls and predicting future needs for health and social services. Sir John thought that the ONS would be the most appropriate body to oversee the repeated standardised surveys necessary, and that it could draw on the extensive experience in the United States in the assessment of disability.

---

[18] OECD: Perceived health status, July 2004.

[19] p 356.

[20] Note of the Seminar, Appendix 4, paragraph 21; Manton KG, Gu X (2001). *Changes in the prevalence of chronic disability in the United States black and nonblack population above age 65 from 1982 to 1999.* Proc Natl Acad Sci USA; 98: 6354-6359.

[21] Appendix 5, paragraph 33.

2.27. Although disability is easier to define, and hence to determine, than ill-health, it is still far from being an absolute. For example, research in the Netherlands has shown that in 85-year olds there can be a marked discrepancy between having an intrinsic capacity to perform an activity of daily living and the translation of this capacity into actually doing it; the factors underlying such a discrepancy may need to be taken into account in measuring "disability".[22] Here too, different countries have different definitions as to what constitutes disability. Australia takes disability to be one or more of 17 defined conditions, Japan takes disability to be confinement to bed, France includes as disabled all those in retirement homes, while in the UK disability is self-reported as a long-standing limitation on activities in any way.[23]

2.28. Despite this, we accept and endorse the view that it is easier to assess disability accurately than it is ill-health, and that disability is less susceptible to changes in people's perceptions of themselves over time. We believe that it is important for all concerned with this question to know more accurately how the health of older people is changing over time; what the trends are; the direction in which and speed with which they are changing; and what the forecasts are for the future.

2.29. **We conclude that there is considerable uncertainty about whether healthy lifespan is increasing faster or slower than lifespan. The uncertainty comes from the variability in individual health trajectories through life, and the difficulty in applying objective measures of health and quality of life across different age groups. We believe that freedom from disability provides a more easily ascertainable objective measure of the quality of life.**

2.30. **Further research should be undertaken to validate and apply appropriate measures to monitor the trends in healthy lifespan. We recommend that funds should be made available to the Office for National Statistics to enable it to carry out over a number of years the surveys needed to assess disability-free life expectancy.**

2.31. If the information provided by such a survey does ultimately show that there is a real increase in the number of years that older people experience ill-health, it will then be possible to look for the causes of that increase, and to attempt to find a remedy. If this is achieved, it will of course improve the quality of life not only of the people concerned, but also of those caring for them. But it will have a further benefit. Some 38% of NHS expenditure is spent on the 16% of the population currently over 65, and a major part of that on the last five years of their lives, whatever the age of death. Anything that can be done to increase the years during which older people are in good health and free from disabilities will therefore additionally free resources which can be used to improve treatment and care of older people.

2.32. For the present, the fact remains that, on any measure, there are a number of years, of the order of eight in the case of men and eleven in the case of women, during which older people regard themselves as not being in general good health, or as having a limiting long-standing illness or disability. Such evidence as there is suggests that this period of perceived ill-health is not

---

[22] A. Bootsma-van der Wiel et al, *Disability in the Oldest Old: "Can Do" or "Do Do"?* (2001) Journal of the American Geriatrics Society, Vol 49, Page 909.

[23] *International Health Comparisons*, National Audit Office, 2003, quoting from OECD Health Data 2002.

decreasing, and may well even be increasing. Perceived ill-health will on its own adversely affect the quality of life of older people, and their sense of well-being.

2.33. The Royal College of Physicians in Edinburgh[24] warned that "Disability may be postponed but it cannot be eliminated". We accept this obvious truth. We accept also that the adverse effects of disability cannot be eliminated. We believe however that it should be possible to increase disability-free years and, if and when disability does supervene, greatly to reduce the adverse effects.

Other factors affecting quality of life

2.34. Older people wish to feel that they are "active providers within the community"(Q 41),[25] that they are a useful part of society, and that they are not a burden on others. This is more likely to be achieved by people who live in their own homes, and who are sufficiently mobile to have access to family, friends and shops. Reasonably good health is undoubtedly a major contributing factor, but it is not the only one. There are ways of ensuring that, although health worsens, quality of life does not, or not at least to the same extent. Technological advances are at the forefront of such measures.

2.35. The focus of this report is therefore to make recommendations which may, first, help to increase HLE, and secondly which may, if and when health does deteriorate, ensure that the quality if life is adversely affected as little as possible. Sir John Grimley Evans summed this up as "Live longer, die faster".[26]

The Need for Longitudinal Studies of Ageing

2.36. The figures obtained from sources such as the Census and the General Household Survey are based on samples taken at a given time, and provide useful snapshots of the position at that time for that sample. Longitudinal studies, on the other hand, aim to follow the changing fortunes of individuals over the years, and thus provide continuing patterns of data, albeit based on smaller samples, from which it may be easier to discern the factors that are responsible for underlying trends. We consider this further in Chapter 7.[27]

---

[24] p 391.

[25] From the evidence of Professor Christopher Phillipson, p 23.

[26] Note of the Seminar, Appendix 4, paragraph 21.

[27] Paragraphs 7.36 – 7.43.

CHAPTER 3: UNDERSTANDING THE AGEING PROCESS

Introduction

3.1.   The timeliness of our inquiry derives not only from the dramatically changing demography, reviewed in Chapter 2, but also from recent advances in the biological understanding of the ageing process. Scientific research on ageing, including research within the UK, has revealed significant new insights into how and why we age, and what might be done to improve the prospects for healthy ageing. This research is overturning many aspects of what might be termed the "traditional" view of ageing. It is also helping us to understand why, contrary to previous expectation, human life expectancy is continuing to increase.

3.2.   In this chapter we consider the natural ageing processes, and in the following chapter those diseases which are particularly prevalent in old age. Not everyone agrees that there is a clear distinction between the two, or that it is helpful to attempt to draw such a distinction. For the reasons given later in this chapter[28] we believe that, at least for the purposes of this report, such a distinction is useful.

The Ageing Process

3.3.   From a biological perspective, ageing is commonly defined in terms of what it does to an organism's vitality and prospects for further survival. Typically, biological gerontologists—those who study the biological mechanisms of ageing—define ageing as "a progressive, generalized impairment of function resulting in a loss of adaptive response to stress and an increasing probability of death".[29] For humans, the underlying pattern of increase in mortality rates shown by the exponential curve in Figure 3, demonstrates that once a person attains adulthood, the annual risk of dying approximately doubles with every 8 additional years that pass.

3.4.   Perhaps the first lesson to draw from these figures is that the common public perception of ageing as something which afflicts only older people, and those approaching old age, is a fallacy. Ageing begins at birth. The increase in the rate of ageing begins at puberty. If this were more widely understood, two consequences might follow. First, if younger people understood that they too are members of a cohort which is ageing at a progressively faster rate, this might have an impact on their frequently ageist attitude to older people. The second consequence is that this younger cohort might learn earlier what can be done—and what they can do—to promote good health and slow the ageing process.

3.5.   Not all creatures age. There are some animals, such as the freshwater *Hydra*, for which the mortality rate does not increase with the passage of time. Thus, ageing is not an absolute biological necessity. As for why species like our own are subject to the inevitability of ageing, the commonly held view has been that ageing is, in effect, biologically programmed by some inner mechanism that imposes a strict upper limit to the lifespan. Were this view to prove

---

[28]   Paragraphs 3.54 to end.

[29]   Professor John Maynard Smith, *The Causes of Ageing*, Proceedings of the Royal Society, 1962.

FIGURE 3

Changes in Mortality Rates

Deaths per thousand population per year, by age and sex. The lower graph shows the same figures plotted on a logarithmic scale. This highlights the fact that for both sexes mortality rates increase exponentially, following the minimum which occurs around the age of puberty and a brief period of excess mortality from accidental causes occurring during young adulthood (ages 18-26).

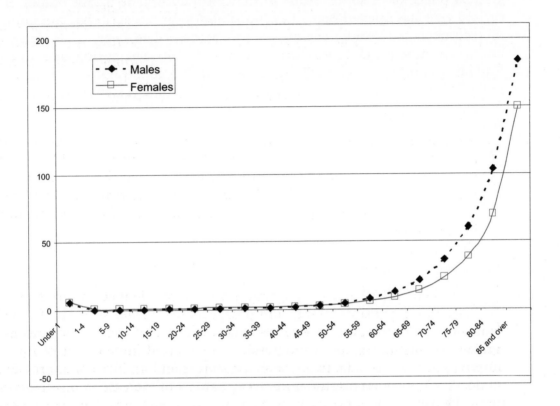

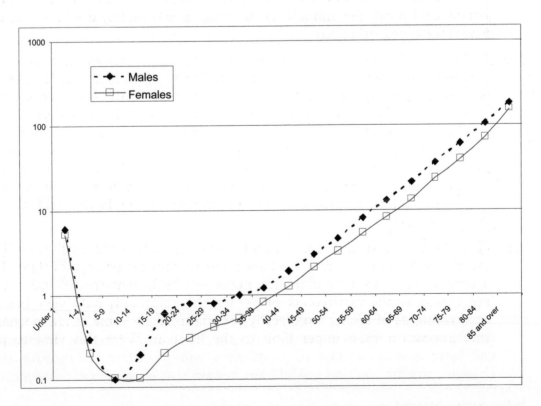

correct, there would be little that could be done to modify the ageing process, unless some means could be found to alter the mechanisms programming our death.

3.6. However, the traditional view that the ageing process is actively programmed by some kind of self-destruct mechanism has been abandoned by most biological gerontologists in favour of the idea that ageing is caused by a gradual build-up of subtle faults in the cells and organs of our bodies. This revised view has opened many new possibilities for research that can improve the prospects for healthy ageing. As will be described later, it also provides important new insights into the relationship between ageing and disease. Equally importantly, it challenges the widespread fatalism that tends to prejudice our ideas about growing old. To some extent the view that deterioration with age is inevitable seems to be a self-fulfilling prophecy. We were told:

"Surprisingly, the age-related decline in physical fitness appears to be more related to expectation than to biology. As we age, we expect to be less fit, so we exercise less, worry less about weight gain, and attempt less demanding roles."[30]

Our Seminar

3.7. We began our inquiry with a seminar held on 14 September 2004 and attended by a number of distinguished participants. A full note of the proceedings is in Appendix 4.

3.8. Professor Kirkwood explained that life expectancy was influenced by a number of factors. Genetic heritability accounted for about 25% of the differences between individuals, with longevity tending to run in families and monozygotic twins having lifespans more similar to each other than dizygotic twins. However, the ageing process was not itself genetically programmed—there are no genes for ageing—but was caused by an accumulation of cellular defects resulting from random molecular damage, with genes influencing cellular repair. Other factors affecting ageing were nutrition, lifestyle and environment, each of which has the potential to modify the rate of accumulation of damage by influencing the body's exposure to intrinsic or extrinsic sources of molecular damage, or by acting upon the body's natural mechanisms for maintenance and repair. These non-genetic factors were in turn amenable to influence by socio-economic factors, as could be seen from variations in life span recorded by different local authorities. In a similar way, the concept of ageing as damage allows the continuing increases in LE to be explained, if the improving conditions within many present-day societies mean that our bodies are accumulating damage more slowly.

3.9. Professor Steve Jackson, from the Gurdon Institute, Cambridge University, addressed the role of damage in ageing further when he considered what ageing was; why and how we aged; whether we could slow down or prevent ageing.

3.10. The symptoms of ageing are a matter of common observation. They consist, among other things, of a loss of vigour; in skin, a loss of the subcutaneous fat cell layer leading to loss of suppleness and wrinkling; connective tissue changes; greying hair and loss of hair; impairment of the senses; osteoporosis;

---

[30] QinetiQ, from research on service personnel, p 381.

and cardiovascular and neurological degeneration. The underlying changes are cellular damage leading to impaired cell function; accumulated tissue and organ damage leading to dysfunction; and the loss of ability for tissue renewal. What we call "ageing" is the intrinsic accumulation of such damage.

3.11. Many matters will influence longevity, but essentially the reason we have not evolved to live longer is that evolution acts to maximise reproductive success, rather than longevity. There is little selective pressure to evolve genes which might allow an individual to live significantly longer than it was likely to survive in the wild, where death usually occurs from accidental causes long before ageing becomes apparent. On the contrary, evolution will select genetic factors which increase reproductive fitness even though this may well cause accelerated ageing.

3.12. Oxidative stress[31] is a major factor causing ageing, and a major target for oxidative damage is DNA. Laboratory animals bred through artificial selection to live longer are those which are more resistant to biochemical stresses such as oxidative stress. The reason calorie restriction tends to enhance the life-span of many organisms is related to its effects on oxidative metabolism and stress-resistance.

3.13. Most human cells can divide only a limited number of times, and when they reach the end of their replication capacity, they enter into senescence. There is evidence that cell senescence also takes place during the ageing of a person. Telomeres, the protective structures at the ends of chromosomes (sometimes likened to the plastic tips that prevent a shoelace from unravelling), shorten over time as a result of oxidative stress. Telomeres in cells thus provide a mechanism to limit cell division: when the telomeres became too short, senescence is induced. There are strong links between telomere shortening and DNA damage. Another link to DNA damage is Werner's syndrome, an autosomal recessive disorder which leads to death in the fourth to sixth decade of life.

3.14. As well as the limitation on cell division capacity, many human cells, such as brain or muscle cells, are essentially post-mitotic (that is, they have attained a specialised state that is unlikely or unable to undergo further division). In these types of cells ageing and death tend to occur not through telomere shortening but through the build up of other types of fault, such as abnormal, damaged proteins. When a cell does not divide, its capacity to clear damage is mainly dependent on turnover ("garbage" disposal and recycling processes), and these appear to become gradually overwhelmed.

3.15. The impressions we gained about the basic biology of ageing during our seminar were borne out during subsequent examination of detailed scientific aspects of ageing, which included a visit to the United States National Institute on Aging.[32] It was clear that in terms of understanding how and why we age, there is a broad consensus among biological gerontologists. However, it was also clear that this is relatively new science being conducted by a number of researchers which is small when compared with more established

---

[31] Oxidative stress is caused by highly reactive molecules called "reactive oxygen species", (ROS) popularly known as "free radicals". ROS are formed chiefly as by-products of the cell's requirement for oxygen, which is used to generate the chemical energy needed to power bodily functions. ROS can damage any structure within the cell, whether proteins, membranes, chromosomal DNA, mitochondrial DNA or telomeres.

[32] A full account of this visit is at Appendix 5.

fields such as cancer or cardiovascular disease. When looking beyond the present areas of knowledge, there is a vast amount yet to be discovered. Not least of the difficulties is the integration of the many different factors and mechanisms that impact upon the ageing process.

Implications of the scientific understanding of ageing

3.16. The implications of the realisation that ageing is caused by lifelong accumulation of molecular and cellular damage, rather than by some rigid inner "clock", are profound. In particular it can be seen, first that the ageing process is more malleable than has been generally appreciated, and secondly that the mechanisms governing health in old age are at work throughout life. This view also has implications for concepts of "normal" ageing and for the perceived value of trying to draw clear scientific distinctions between intrinsic ageing and age-related diseases. We consider this question later in this chapter.[33]

3.17. Intrinsic malleability of the ageing process is evident in the changes that are continuing to occur in LE, long after the major gains that were brought about from the control of infectious diseases (particularly those which killed the young during the 19th and first half of the 20th centuries) were essentially complete. What is driving the current increase in LE is a decline in death rates among older people, including the oldest old (those over 85 years). It is perhaps an unreliable commonplace to observe that "70 is the new 50", but we are all aware that, on average, today's cohorts of older people are different from their predecessors. It is this apparent malleability of the ageing process that gives scientific basis to the hope expressed in Chapter 2, that it may be possible to reduce the expectation of unhealthy years of life, even while LE itself is increasing.

3.18. The importance of recognising that ageing begins in youth cannot be overstated. Indeed, from what we are learning about the underlying mechanisms of ageing, the build up of molecular and cellular damage probably starts *in utero*. The evidence that genetic factors account for just 25% of human longevity suggests that much can be gained from targeting the non-genetic factors such as nutrition, lifestyle and environment as early as possible.

3.19. It is as yet unclear how far the intrinsic malleability of the ageing process can be exploited. This is a matter for future research. In order to slow the accumulation of molecular and cellular damage that underpins the ageing, the immediate targets are those that are already known to affect damage and repair, while it is in principle possible that future interventions using drugs or stem cells might open new avenues. This plainly raises the question whether extending the human life-span would in fact be beneficial for the individual, and desirable for the individual or for society as a whole. These are not matters we have considered; to do so would have unacceptably broadened the scope of our inquiry. We do however note that, in marked contrast to the perennial fascination of the media with the idea that science might discover the secret of eternal youth, none of those we have consulted suggested that an aim of scientific research should be to seek to extend the human life-span (as opposed to eliminating factors which shorten it). Indeed, among the many experts on diseases and disabilities of ageing to whom we have listened,

---

[33] Paragraphs 3.55 to end.

there have been few who have even referred to the possible benefits of stem cell therapies. These therapies are frequently promoted as having the potential to treat and even cure age-related pathology; we suspect that realistic progress down this route is as yet uncertain and at best some way off.

Factors that promote good health and slow the ageing process

3.20. Age Concern England summarised what appears to be a consensus view when they told us that the factors that promote good health and slow the ageing process are—

- physical activity;

- having a social role and function;

- good nutrition;

- absence of risk factors such as smoking and drinking to excess; and

- good mental health and well-being.[34]

We consider each of these factors in turn.

Physical activity

3.21. Those of our witnesses who addressed this were unanimous in believing that physical activity is a key to predicting independence and mortality in later life. Disability and infirmity may be largely the result of disuse of muscle rather than the inevitable process of ageing.[35] The Royal College of Physicians of Edinburgh agreed: "Physical activity is the major modifiable influence on health in old age."[36] The Royal Society of Edinburgh explained that "exercise can positively affect peak bone mass in children and adolescents, has been shown to help maintain or even modestly increase bone density in adulthood, and can assist in minimizing age related bone loss in older adults."[37]

3.22. After age 40 we lose muscle mass at about one to 2% per year. A comparison of athletes and non-athletes in their 70s shows that their rate of loss is the same, but the athletes start from a higher standard. The rate of muscle loss can be influenced by strengthening exercise programmes. A three-month exercise programme can rejuvenate muscle mass by a 15-year equivalent. By starting early enough it is possible to raise the threshold at which we can influence those inevitable age-related changes (Q 346).[38] Recent evidence has shown that community-based exercise training programmes for healthy older people can have profound effects in reversing muscle wasting and the accompanying functional deficit.[39] Lost fitness can be regained with regular activity even in extreme old age.[40]

---

[34] p 274.

[35] Age Concern, p 274.

[36] p 392.

[37] p 390.

[38] From the evidence of Professor Rose Anne Kenny, Professor of Geriatric Medicine in the University of Newcastle-upon-Tyne, p 178.

[39] Biosciences Federation, p 330.

[40] Royal College of Physicians of Edinburgh, p 393.

3.23. It comes as no surprise to find strong evidence that dog ownership leads to substantial increases in physical exercise. A study of new pet-owners in 1990 found that new dog-owners "displayed a dramatic increase in the number/duration of walks taken after the first month, and this increase was maintained both to six months and to ten months". At the end of the study, dog-owners reported that increased exercise was one of the most important differences made to them, second only to increased companionship and affection.[41]

3.24. Two cautionary notes need to be sounded when advocating the benefits of exercise. First, although the beneficial effects of exercise are clear, there may be adverse effects, particularly on the joints, of too much physical wear; these effects can be mitigated by choosing which kinds of exercise to undertake and by taking appropriate precautions, such as wearing suitable shoes for running. Second, extreme exercise such as is undertaken by world class athletes appears sometimes to accelerate age-related degeneration of muscle cells, probably through over-use. However for most of us, even though exercise temporarily increases metabolic rate and thereby the potential to suffer oxidative damage, this appears to be more than compensated by stimulating the body's repair and antioxidant defence systems.

3.25. **Local authorities can do much to help people of all ages, including older people, to benefit from exercise. Facilities for cycling are often poor or non-existent; sometimes even walking is a perilous activity. Local authorities should aim to improve facilities for exercise; they should make it their business to inform older people about these facilities; they should encourage them to use these facilities; and they should ensure that adequate transport is available.**

3.26. In the longer term, it is plain that increase in exercise during the school years will have a beneficial effect throughout life, and that the benefits will be particularly felt in old age. It is therefore a matter of concern to us that more is not being done to reverse the selling off of school playing fields and the consequent reduction in school sports. Since October 1998, when section 77 of the School Standards and Framework Act 1998 came into force, such sales have required the consent of the Secretary of State for Education. However, since that consent is withheld only in a very small proportion of cases,[42] this has slowed but not halted the sale of playing fields. In August 2004 the then Secretary of State stated that the rules were being tightened up, and that the sale of a playing field "must be an absolute last resort". We hope that future figures will bear this out.

3.27. DCMS figures show that in 2002 only 25% of 5-16 year olds spent "a minimum of two hours each week on high quality PE and school sport".[43] By July 2004 this proportion had risen to 62%. This trend is in the right direction, but must be continued if we are not to have a generation which, because it had in its youth limited opportunities for physical activity, will as it grows older be increasingly at risk of disability and infirmity. The White

---

[41] J.A. Serpell, *Beneficial aspects of pet ownership on some aspects of human health and behaviour*, Journal of the Royal Society of Medicine, 84: 717-720, 1991.

[42] The National Playing Fields Association stated in *Fields Focus*, Spring 2003, that of the disposals of school playing fields scrutinised by the Secretary of State between October 1998 and December 2002, over 97% had been approved.

[43] DCMS Autumn Performance Report, January 2004, Cm 6095.

Paper *Choosing Health,* published in November 2004, states that the national target is to increase this figure from 62% to 75% in 2006 and to 85% in 2008.[44] If these targets are achieved, that will be a very welcome development. But considerably more than two hours a week is needed to make a real difference; we would like to see a further target for a substantial increase in this minimal time.

3.28. **Exercise at all ages is one of the most effective ways to counter the adverse effects of ageing on functional capacity. The Government should publish plans showing how they intend to promote, in schools and elsewhere, the benefits of exercise as a factor contributing to improved health at all ages.**

3.29. **Consent for the disposal of playing fields must be refused unless the facilities lost are to be replaced by sports or exercise facilities which are as good or better.**

Nutrition

3.30. There is very considerable evidence that health in old age is greatly influenced by nutrition earlier in life, in childhood, and even before birth (QQ 90-91).[45] Since nutrition provides the essential raw materials of life, it is unsurprising that foods can both promote and retard the accumulation of cellular and molecular damage. "Bad" foods include those containing saturated fats, those with a high sugar intake, and substances which may cause DNA damage (it should be noted that some natural substances, including plant materials, can damage DNA, probably as part of the plant's defences). "Good" foods include fruits and vegetables and those containing natural antioxidants, such as fish oils.

3.31. Dr van der Ouderaa explained this further:

"There is very strong data from epidemiology and in particular the excellent EPIC-Norfolk study by the University of Cambridge which shows that high fruit and vegetable nutrition reduced the prevalence of disease by up to 50% for cardiovascular disease and a similar percentage for mortality in the period of eight years that the two studies were done ... However, on the other extreme, if you have someone who chain smokes, has a sedentary life and has high stress shift work, then a couple of pieces of broccoli and two oranges are not going to save this person."(Q 89)

3.32. In order to achieve maximum benefit from healthy nutrition, good habits should be established as early as possible. There is currently considerable concern about the long-term health effects of poor nutrition among school children, with the associated increase in obesity. What is less well understood is that poor nutrition also contributes to an acceleration of features of the underlying ageing process, leading to an increased risk of diabetes, cardiovascular disease and stroke in later life. This can also be caused by insufficient or inadequate nutrition *in utero* (Q 90).

3.33. Professor Elizabeth Kay, who gave evidence to us on behalf of the British Dental Association, explained that nutrition has a double effect on oral health. A person's life time nutrition affects how oral health turns out when

---

[44] Cm 6374, chapter 3, paragraph 70.

[45] From the evidence of Professor John Mathers on behalf of the British Nutrition Foundation and of Dr Frans van der Ouderaa, Vice-President, Corporate Research, Unilever plc, p 40.

they are elderly; it is mostly exposure to sugar and exposure to fluoride that will affect the amount of dental decay in later years. That dental decay will in turn affect whether they have teeth in later years, and loss of a significant number of teeth affects what they are able to eat. Specifically, it reduces the amount of fruit, vegetables and vitamin C they consume, with all the knock-on effects that that may have (Q 89). "In terms of nutrition in oral health there are two things: decrease sugar intake, and have the optimum level of fluoride intake." (Q 111)

3.34. The White Paper *Choosing Health* devotes a chapter to this problem. It states, and we agree, that "it is not for Government to dictate to [people] what they can and cannot consume". The central message is that there is no lack of information about what food is healthy, but that "messages about health are sometimes inconsistent or uncoordinated and out of step with the way people actually live their lives". The paper sees the Government's role as "to help information providers to give factual information that is up to date and accurate". It states that the Government "will press vigorously both before and during the UK presidency of the EU in 2005 to simplify nutrition labelling and make it mandatory on packaged foods". The Government "intends to discuss with the food industry how they might contribute to funding national campaigns to promote positive health information and education".[46]

3.35. We very much welcome and support the approach taken in the White Paper. It is perhaps natural that, at a time of great concern about childhood obesity and the lifestyles of younger people, this chapter is addressed mainly to the needs of the young. It is not only children, however, who have unhealthy diets. Older people too have problems which include inadequate knowledge of appropriate diets, and affordability and availability of healthy foods. They have particular problems with labelling which is not only uninformative, but often in such minute print that it is for practical purposes illegible. We believe that the approach proposed by the Government should not concentrate on the young to the exclusion of the old. The presentation of labelling is as important as its content.

3.36. **Nutrition and oral health have major impacts on health throughout the lifespan. Since a person's health in old age reflects molecular and cellular damage that accumulates throughout life, and since nutrition affects the accumulation of such damage (adversely in the case of poor nutrition, beneficially in the case of good nutrition), the links between healthy eating and healthy ageing need to be better understood and communicated to the public.**

3.37. **We welcome and commend the approach of the White Paper *Choosing Health*, and the importance it attaches to the provision of information about healthy nutrition. We recommend that this approach should be extended to cover the specific problems of older people.**

---

[46] Cm 6374, Chapter 2, paragraphs 7, 11, 19, 23 and 43. In 2004 the Government spent £7 million on food campaigns; in 2003 the food industry spent £743 million on advertising food, soft drinks and chain restaurants.

Absence of risk factors: smoking, and drinking to excess

3.38. Damage to cells and molecules within the body can be accelerated, sometimes dramatically, by exposure to specific agents, such as tobacco smoke, drugs and excess alcohol. The adverse effects of tobacco smoke are very well known and almost certainly include acceleration of ageing. "Healthy ageing starts with smoking cessation" (Q 125);[47] cigarette smoking "is almost certainly a risk factor for dementia" (Q 327).[48] Maternal smoking is linked to the capacity to transport calcium across the placenta and the foetus and subsequently the infant's capacity to grow, which may also have long-term effects with implications for healthy ageing (Q 51).[49] Relatively little is known as yet about the specific adverse effects of drug abuse and binge drinking on the damage that underlies ageing; however, we would be surprised if such effects are absent.

Having a social role and function

3.39. Long-term population-based studies show that social and productive activities are as important as physical activity in reducing the likelihood of illness and institutionalisation. The mechanisms for these effects are unclear. It is very possible that physical activity is a pre-condition for participation in many social activities, or that it may derive in part from the incidental social and purposeful activity involved. Physical activity may in itself reflect social competence and being in control of one's life. Whatever the mechanism, the two factors are clearly related to better health and the delay of onset of illness.[50]

3.40. It also appears to be the case that, leaving aside the effects of all the factors we have listed above, people with higher social status have better health and longer lives than those of lower status: the social gradient, as it has been called by Professor Sir Michael Marmot, Professor of Epidemiology and Public Health at University College London. Professor Marmot has carried out a number of Whitehall studies which show that the most junior civil servants—clerks and messengers—are significantly more likely to suffer from coronary heart disease and other diseases of old age than senior civil servants. Low status leads to stress; the more one is in control of the situation, the higher on the social ladder one goes, the better one's health is likely to be.[51]

General well-being

3.41. The factors we have listed above will all contribute to the promotion of good health and to slowing the ageing process from the earliest years into old age. There are other factors which, though not unimportant when a person is younger, play a major part in promoting health and longevity in later years. Prominent among these are good housing in a safe and pleasant neighbourhood, and the other environmental matters we mention in Chapter 5. Neighbourhood issues such as crime and antisocial behaviour (or the fear of them), or environmental concerns such as poor paving and litter

---

[47] From the evidence of Dr Frans van der Ouderaa, p 48; and see also paragraphs 3.

[48] From the evidence of Professor Carol Brayne, Professor of Public Health Medicine, Cambridge, p 170.

[49] From the evidence of Professor Cyrus Cooper, Professor of Rheumatology, University of Southampton, p30.

[50] Age Concern England, p 274.

[51] Michael Marmot, *Status Syndrome*, published by Bloomsbury, June 2004.

which can lead to falls, can prevent older people from leaving their houses. This reduces opportunities for social interaction with family and friends, and this in turn can impact on mental and physical health.

3.42. We note that the Wanless Report shares our view as to the importance of promoting those matters which can improve health:

"Better public health measures could significantly affect the demand for health care. A number of respondents emphasised that, while much of the beneficial impact might occur beyond the end of the 20-year period, that should not prevent action being taken in the short term ... Others said that investment in changing people's behaviour now, such as cutting out smoking, improving diet and encouraging more exercise, could significantly improve the populations' health status."[52]

Variability and diversity

Individuality of the ageing process

3.43. In our seminar, Professor Kirkwood drew attention to a curious feature of the ageing process, namely the individuality of how it affects us. We know that one day we will die, but we generally have little advance warning of how long we will live or what we will die from. We have seen that genes, nutrition, lifestyle and socioeconomic factors all play a part, but in addition to these there is a significant degree of variability in the ageing process. As Professor Kirkwood showed, this variability is seen even within populations of genetically identical animals raised under conditions of extreme uniformity. To some extent such variability is inevitable, given that ageing is driven ultimately by the accumulation of damage, which will not follow an identical course even in identical twins.

3.44. Recognising the individuality of ageing is important at many levels. The general deterioration of the human body with age, and the consequent increase of frailty, is well documented. However, the extent and underlying causes of individuality are less well known. Box 3 gives the findings of the 2002 English Longitudinal Study of Ageing (ELSA).

---

[52] Final Report of the Review by Derek Wanless, *Securing our Future Health: Taking a Long-Term View*, April 2002, paragraph 1.27.

BOX 3

Variations in Physical Impairment

There is considerable variation in the level of physical impairment between age groups. The prevalence of reported physical functional limitation is surprisingly high at the youngest end of the sample, with 43% of respondents in their 50s reporting difficulty with mobility, and 13% reporting difficulty with a basic activity of daily life (self-care). At the same time, most (58%) of the respondents in their 80s and older report no difficulties with basic activities of daily life, and 17% report no difficulty with mobility functions

The variation in the level of impairment by occupational class is also considerable. Respondents with routine and manual occupations report up to twice as many difficulties with physical function as those with managerial or professional occupations. This occupational class disability gap is equivalent to the disability gap between age groups 10-15 years or more apart

Walking speed slows dramatically with age. Only around one in forty people aged between 60 and 64 walk more slowly than 0.4 metres/second, compared with one in five at age 80 and over. This deterioration in walking speed is more marked in women than in men.[53]

3.45. The current publicly accepted view is undoubtedly that deterioration over time is inevitable, and that it is only the rate of deterioration which differs between individuals. For example, hearing impairment has long been viewed as an inevitable consequence of growing old, not only among the medical profession but also by the man in the street, so that very often people do not complain about it as much as they should as they grow older (Q 342).[54] The same applies to incontinence, a disabling and distressing condition which, according to Help the Aged,[55] is suffered by 6 million people of all ages in the UK.

3.46. Measuring individual differences in ageing rate remains an important challenge, for which there is as yet no entirely satisfactory solution. We talk about people being "old before their time", and we envy those who, though in their eighties, not only enter the London Marathon, but finish it. These are extreme examples, but the fact remains that their bodies have aged at different rates—sometimes startlingly different. If we want to be able to understand the factors that affect ageing rate, we need better tools to measure individual differences in this rate. The measurements provided by such procedures are often described as "biomarkers" of ageing. They are particularly important if we want to measure the impact of interventions that might slow ageing rates without having to wait decades to determine their effectiveness. A biomarker provides an indication of a person's biological age (that is, how far, in bodily terms, they are on the journey from birth to death), as distinct from chronological age which merely measures the number of years they have lived.

---

[53] ELSA, summary of chapter 7. 0.4 metres/second is less than 1 mph.

[54] From the evidence of Professor Karen Steel, Principal Investigator, Wellcome Trust Sanger Institute, p 177.

[55] p 280.

3.47. **In the light of improved knowledge of underlying biological mechanisms and the need to measure the efficacy of interventions aimed at improving healthy ageing, we recommend that specific attention be given to funding research on biomarkers of ageing.**

Distinctions in the ageing process between the sexes

3.48. If evidence were needed that the ageing processes in men and women are different, it is provided by the statistics set out in Chapter 2 and by the mortality data shown in Figure 3. These reveal the markedly higher life expectancy of women, with lower age-specific mortality at all ages, but also their greater unhealthy life expectancy. There has been much speculation about the underlying causes for the difference in LE between men and women. Some argue that the difference is behavioural, and that as women increasingly adopt work and lifestyle patterns similar to those of men, the difference will diminish. However, in animal studies it has been shown that cells from female rats are intrinsically better protected against oxidative stress than cells from male rats, suggesting that the difference may be more biological. Biological differences between the sexes that impact on ageing, such as the difference in antioxidant protection, appear to be regulated at least partly by sex hormones. For example, there is some evidence from animal studies (and even some for humans) that male castration reduces or eliminates the lifespan difference between the sexes.

Distinctions between social groups

3.49. We explained in paragraph 2.10 the contribution made by differences in social class to the very marked differences in life expectancy between local authority areas which in some cases are separated by no more than a few miles. Commonly assigned reasons for this are, as we have explained,[56] poor nutrition and smoking (including of the mother during pregnancy), but also sub-standard housing, child poverty, and teenage pregnancies. All of these are factors which will increase the risk of ill-health and disease, not just in old age, but throughout the lifespan; and they are all factors which were considered by Sir Donald Acheson in his 1998 report on Health Inequalities.[57] General ill-health is outside our remit, but ill-health in early life will of course adversely affect health in old age. To this extent therefore we have included it in our deliberations. We agree with Professor Christopher Phillipson that there are great differences in the quality of life people will achieve in old age, and that this cannot be resolved when people are already old (Q 33).

3.50. Social advantages do sometimes have attendant disadvantages. A recent study[58] has shown that, while there appears to be no difference in bone mass between children from different social classes, those from Social Class I are, by age 10, on average 1.5cm taller and 1kg lighter than those from Social Class V. Their bones therefore tend to be longer and more slender, and this appears to make them more vulnerable to fractures or osteoporosis in later life.

---

[56] Paragraphs 3.30 and 3.38.

[57] Sir Donald Acheson, *Independent Inquiry into Inequalities in Health*, part 1 (The Stationery Office, 1998).

[58] By Dr Emma Clark, based on the Avon Longitudinal Study of Parents and Children.

Distinctions between ethnic groups

3.51. We explained in the previous chapter that the difficulties involved in attempting to isolate the individual factors which contribute to a lower life expectancy among lower social groups are even more acute in the case of ethnic minorities. It nevertheless appears that on all health indicators, Pakistani and Bangladeshi elders and, to a lesser extent, Indian and Black Caribbean elders, are more likely to report ill-health, and that the ethnic differences remain even after allowance has been made for differences in material resources.[59]

3.52. The underlying biological reasons for ageing do not appear to differ between different ethnic groups. Thus, "a recent Canadian study showed that, although the *prevalence* of heart disease varied greatly in the 52 countries examined, the actual *causes* of disease (e.g. hypertension, diabetes, smoking, alcohol, abnormal lipids) did not differ."[60]

3.53. We also received evidence from the Policy Research Institute on Ageing and Ethnicity (PRIAE), which seeks to improve the health and quality of life of black and minority ethnic (BME) elders at national and European level.[61] From this evidence it is clear that the incidence of hypertension is higher among middle-aged South Asians and African Caribbeans than among the overall population; yet while there is a substantially higher incidence of CHD among South Asians, the incidence among African Caribbeans is lower than the national average. It is however not easy to determine to what extent this is influenced by factors such as diet, lifestyle and socio-economic circumstances, and what contribution is made by genuine ethnic and genetic differences. But these differences undoubtedly exist. Dr Frans van der Ouderaa told us that if one compared three ethnic groups—the Chinese, the Indian and the Malays—in Singapore, it appeared that in a high stress urbanised environment Asian Indians became diabetic about fifteen years before the Chinese and about ten years before the Malays (Q 132). There is some indication that populations may become adapted to prevailing nutritional patterns and that if these patterns are altered, either through changing economic circumstances or through migration, this may have important effects on health.[62]

3.54. Since submitting their evidence to us, PRIAE published in December 2004 their report of a study into Minority Elder Care in ten European countries. This includes statistics showing marked differences in the incidence of a range of medical problems among black and minority ethnic elders in the UK.

[59] Maria Evandrou, *Ethnic Inequalities in Health in Later Life,* Health Statistics Quarterly 08, Winter 2000.

[60] Academy of Medical Sciences, p 193.

[61] p 372.

[62] Bateson et al, *Developmental Plasticity and Human Health,* Nature 430, 22 July 2004.

TABLE 4

Medical Problems of Black and Minority Ethnic Elders

	African-Caribbean %	South Asian %	Chinese/Vietnamese %
Arthritis/rheumatism	45	61	55
High blood pressure	64	57	38
Diabetes	40	38	17
Heart disease	24	33	10
Lung/breathing problem	14	26	15
Osteoporosis	5	13	21
Kidney problems	4	18	15

Note: numbers refer to per cent of each group referring to a particular problem

The relationship between ageing and disease

3.55. A question of immense significance is the distinction between the natural ageing processes, and those diseases which are particularly prevalent in old age. The Medical Research Council (MRC), the Department of Health (DoH) and the Wellcome Trust all told us that they directed most of their attention within the field towards diseases and disabilities, with relatively little focus on the ageing process itself. In contrast, the Biotechnology and Biological Sciences Research Council (BBSRC) focused on underpinning mechanisms of ageing and not directly on diseases.

3.56. Within the United States, we heard from the National Institute on Aging that they drew a distinction between the two areas, but found funding research into specific diseases much easier; much of their research was therefore disease-related. On the other hand the Ellison Medical Foundation, a private foundation investing $20 million annually on ageing, concentrated more on basic research. Dr Richard Sprott, the Executive Director of the Foundation, told us he felt that the funding of research was too much orientated towards research into diseases, to the exclusion of the basic underlying science.

3.57. Although we could understand the reasons why different organisations should focus more on ageing or on disease, we quickly discovered that the distinction is not always a clear one. Professor Cyrus Cooper, who gave evidence to us on behalf of the National Osteoporosis Society and the Arthritis Research Campaign, explained that this was particularly true in the rheumatological arena. Bone mineral density and the thickness of the cartilage of the joint changed with age, leading to an increasing risk of the likelihood of the adverse health event: fractures and osteoporosis, joint pain, disability and osteoarthritis. The original approaches to definition simply picked the threshold at which it was felt that the risk of disease became unacceptably high, and set the definition at that point. Definitions were now more sophisticated, but there was still no very clear distinction between gradual deterioration with age, and the stage at which it was appropriate to say that a person was suffering from a disease (Q 47).

3.58. Furthermore, it may sometimes be difficult and unhelpful to distinguish between age-related diseases and the deterioration which results from them. It seems to us that whilst specific diseases and disabilities are the manifestations of growing older, there are underlying basic processes that inevitably age us which are to be found in the mechanisms contributing to the accumulation of molecular and cellular damage. In the words of Professor Linda Partridge, Weldon Professor of Biometry, University College London, "what we are looking at is an underlying process of progressive loss of function that leads to increasing vulnerability to various diseases... there is an underlying ageing process that can affect all these diseases simultaneously" (Q 387).

3.59. However in the majority of fields, witnesses thought that a helpful distinction could be drawn. The Royal College of Physicians of Edinburgh agreed that "the crucial distinction between the effects of age alone and the effects of disease require[s] to be reinforced in the minds of both the lay public and health professionals".[63]

3.60. Professor Clive Ballard, Director of Research at the Alzheimer's Society, supported this view:

"It is not ageing itself that causes the problems but the diseases that become more common with ageing. If you look at the age of a particular population then the risk of particular conditions will be higher, but that is because the underlying factors that contribute to these conditions become higher rather than that age itself causes problems *per se*." (Q 308)

3.61. Dr van der Ouderaa said: "I think it is helpful to discriminate between age related diseases and ageing as separate processes from a communication point of view." However, he qualified this by going on to say: "I think a lot of the etiological factors are actually quite similar"(Q 123). Professor Mathers agreed and added: "I tend to think of the ageing process as a process in which our ability to cope with perturbations of the norm become more and more difficult. The ability to maintain homeostasis, if you like, becomes more difficult so we need to be able to defend that state, and ageing is a way in which we begin to lose that ability." (Q 124)

3.62. There does seem to be a widely held perception of such a distinction, which has implications both for finding the path to scientific understanding and for attitudes. For example, in the case of cardiovascular disease, if it proves possible to prevent atherosclerosis (hardening of the arteries) from occurring, the age-related increase in heart disease and stroke will be greatly reduced. Whether this will entirely eliminate circulatory problems that develop with age is less certain, however, and it may be that in order to prevent atherosclerosis we will need to understand why older arteries are intrinsically more vulnerable to atherosclerosis that young ones.

3.63. In terms of attitude, diseases are regarded as being susceptible of a cure, and deserving of sympathy. Ageing is thought of as the general lot of mankind, and as something which must be endured. This affects public attitudes—it is much easier to raise funds for research on specific diseases—and it also affects the attitudes of professionals. For many doctors, whose motivation is to cure disease, we suspect that ageing too often has undertones of failure.

3.64. We believe that there are three reasons to be cautious about accepting too readily a distinction between ageing and disease. First, for most age-related diseases, age itself is the single largest risk factor, so to try to research the disease without also addressing the underlying process of ageing seems ill-advised. It may simply be impossible to combat the one without the other.

---

[63] p 392.

3.65. The view that ageing is driven by an accumulation of cellular and molecular damage is not very different from the view of the mechanisms responsible for most if not all age-related diseases, so there is great potential for specific age-related diseases to share common causative mechanisms not only with ageing itself but also with other age-related diseases.

3.66. Finally, attempts to maintain a distinction between ageing and disease are likely to work to the disadvantage of those who are not "fortunate" enough to have a clearly recognised disease and who "merely" suffer from the multiple conditions that tend to afflict older people.

3.67. **Most of the research on ageing and health within the UK is focused on specific diseases and medical conditions for which age is the single largest risk factor. However, there is little research on underpinning mechanisms of such diseases which may be linked to basic processes of ageing. The Department of Health and other medical research funders, including the major charities, should develop and implement strategies to address links between ageing and disease.**

3.68. In this chapter, we have considered the intrinsic processes of ageing. In the following chapter we explore more closely age-related diseases and disorders.

CHAPTER 4: AGE-RELATED DISEASES AND DISORDERS

Introduction

4.1. During this inquiry we have received written and oral evidence from those involved in improving understanding of the major age-related diseases. In this chapter we examine the most important conditions affecting older people on which we have taken evidence. We look at their effect, what treatment is available now and being investigated, and how they interact with other ageing processes. Finally we turn our attention to the interaction between age-related diseases and underlying ageing processes, and how they are both funded.

Conditions affecting older people

4.2. We saw in Chapter 3 how the age-specific mortality rates in men and women increase very sharply with age. Since death is usually preceded by illness, it will be no surprise that many of the conditions affecting older people show similar sharp increases with age. The fact that illness becomes very much more prevalent with age has led to widespread concern that the increasing numbers of older people will necessarily result in dramatic increases in the costs of healthcare. However, for most people the major lifetime healthcare costs are associated with terminal illness, and this has greatly exaggerated the impression that old age is itself driving up healthcare costs. Everyone is likely to incur such costs regardless of how long they live, but most of us can now expect to incur them in old age. As Sir John Grimley Evans told us:

"The costs in the last five years of life do not derive from predictably futile treatment but from treatments doctors hope will be curative or palliative. With present levels of life expectancy most people experiencing what will prove to be their final illness are aged over 75. This can give the impression that high costs of health care are due to age rather than to being ill, and that any increase in numbers of older people due to lengthening of lifespan will increase NHS expenditure disproportionately. This is not so."[64]

4.3. Increasing healthcare costs are however likely to arise if the prevalence of chronic age-related conditions rises and if the average duration of these conditions lengthens. For this reason it is important not only to have better information about trends in HLE, as noted in Chapter 2, but also to learn as much as possible about the causes and treatment prospects for conditions affecting older people.

4.4. In terms of mortality, the three major causes of death, each responsible for more than 10% of all deaths in those aged over 65, are:

- circulatory diseases,

- respiratory diseases, and

- cancer.

The age profile (Figure 4) shows that it is the first two of these which grow most significantly with age. The proportion of deaths from cancer is less age-dependent, being a significant cause at any age.

---

[64] p 357.

FIGURE 4

Major Causes of Death by Age

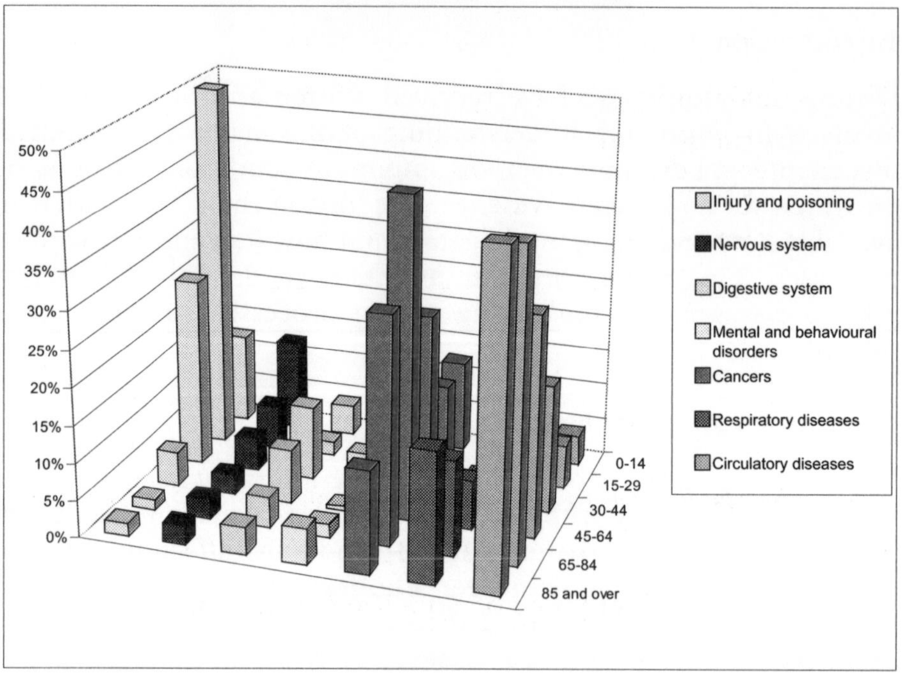

The major causes of death by age. Columns represent the proportion of deaths in that age group due to each disease/disorder.

4.5. Rates of chronic sickness increase as we get older.[65] The five most prevalent conditions affecting more than 5% of the population over 65 involve:

- the heart and circulatory system (including heart attack and stroke);

- the musculoskeletal system;

- endocrine and metabolic functions (including diabetes);

- the respiratory system; and

- the digestive system.

Over the age of 75 eye and ear complaints also become important.

4.6. Whilst the incidence of all of these conditions in the general population increases with age, those affecting the heart and circulatory system, and eye and ear complaints, stand out as striking older people in particular.

---

[65] General Household Survey 2003, table 7.13

FIGURE 5

Increases in Longstanding Conditions

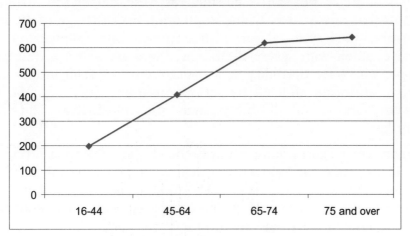

Rate per thousand reporting one or more longstanding conditions at specific ages

FIGURE 6

Incidence of Specific Conditions

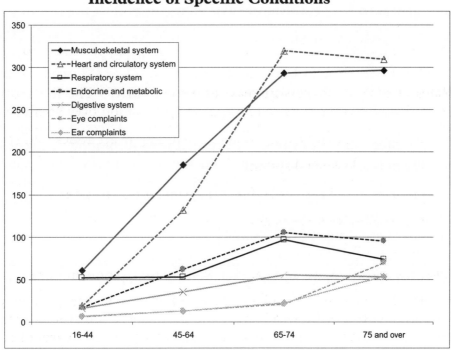

Rate per thousand reporting certain longstanding conditions at specific ages

4.7. Other specific illnesses affecting predominantly older people include dementia and Parkinson's disease. Both affect about one person in a thousand under the age of 65, and increase with age. Dementia, including Alzheimer's disease, rises to affect 25% of those over 85 (Q 305);[66] Parkinson's disease is less common, affecting around 2% of those over 70.

Stroke

4.8. A stroke comes from an interruption of blood supply to the brain by either a blood clot in an artery (an ischaemic stroke, the most common form) or a

---

[66] From the evidence of Professor Carol Brayne, p165.

burst blood vessel in the brain (a haemorrhagic stroke). About 125,000 people each year in the UK have a stroke, 90% of whom are over 55. Professor Peter Fentem, Chairman of Research of the Stroke Association, told us that one quarter of the population over the age of 45 will suffer from a stroke. Each year about 70,000 people die following a stroke. Many survive, albeit with severe disabilties: there are about a quarter of a million people who have disability as a consequence of their stroke and those who survive are often affected by serious disability (Q 272). "Stroke is a more powerful cause of disability than musculoskeletal and other chronic disorders".[67]

4.9. Twenty years ago nothing could be done to heal a stroke, but progress from medical science has led to fewer deaths, and less disability for those who do survive.[68] However, we have been disappointed to learn of the UK's poor record in the treatment of stroke compared with other countries. Professor Fentem informed us that the mortality rate in the UK 30 days after a stroke is 30%, compared with less than 15% in Canada (Q 278). We also note a European study from 1999 which found "significant differences in 3-month outcome in terms of case fatality or dependency for stroke that are unexplained by conventional case mix variable adjustment. The UK centers also appear to have consistently worse outcomes than the rest of Europe."[69]

4.10. We understood from both Professor Kennedy Lees, Professor of Cerebrovascular Medicine at the University of Glasgow, and Professor Fentem that brain imaging (with MRI or CT scans) immediately a stroke has been diagnosed will improve patient outcomes; countries like Germany and Canada have a far higher proportion of patients making a good recovery. Professor Lees told us that if imaging detected an ischaemic stroke within three hours of its onset, treatment with thrombolytic drugs could have a significant effect by restoring blood supply to areas of the brain. He added that even beyond three hours, imaging would detect salvageable tissue and might allow direct treatment. There are, though, "only half a dozen" centres in the UK that have the rapid access to scanners required for stroke patients, and use these drugs (QQ 276-279).

4.11. Professor Fentem noted the Royal College of Physicians' guidelines on stroke which state that brain imaging "should be undertaken as soon as possible in all patients, at least within 24 hours of onset". However, in its National Sentinel Stroke Audit 2004, the Royal College of Physicians found that "only 47% of the patients had a scan performed within two calendar days of the stroke."[70]

4.12. **Stroke is a major cause of long-term illness, disability and death, particularly among older people. Yet significant reductions in the long-term health consequences of a stroke can be made if very early assessments and treatments are provided, for example by locating scanners within accident and emergency departments. The Department of Health should make rapid treatment of stroke a priority.**

---

[67] The Stroke Association, p 142.

[68] Professor Ian Philp in the Foreword to *The National Clinical Guidelines for Stroke*, 2nd edition, June 2004.

[69] Wolfe et al, *Variations in Case Fatality and Dependency from Stroke in Western and Central Europe*, American Heart Association, February 1999.

[70] Clinical Effectiveness and Evaluation Unit, Royal College of Physicians, March 2005.

4.13. The National Audit Office, in collaboration with the Stroke Association, is investigating stroke services in England, focusing on whether the NHS is effectively using its resources to prevent stroke, to provide acute care, to manage rehabilitation of stroke patients, and to integrate health and social care services for people who have suffered a stroke. We look forward to their report.

4.14. Regarding expenditure on research on stroke, Professor Lees told us that expenditure in the UK on stroke research is about 1% of that on cancer, despite stroke carrying a very similar, if not worse, prognosis than cancer (Q 276). A study comparing costs of illnesses with research funding put total expenditure on stroke at £9.1 million, about 5% of that on cancer. It estimated the annual cost of stroke to the NHS and social services in England to be £2.5 billion, compared to £1.6 billion for cancer. Across age ranges, stroke is responsible for 11% of all deaths each year, compared to 25% of deaths resulting from cancer.[71]

4.15. Looking ahead 10 or 15 years, Professor Lees saw research opening up the possibility of using stem cells and new drugs to encourage repair mechanisms in the brain. Professor Fentem concentrated on preventative measures, and the importance of lifestyle factors in the development and progress of chronic disease. "A big challenge is going to be to implement Wanless.[72] That will take 20 years" (Q 300).

Heart

4.16. Coronary heart disease (CHD) results from artery walls becoming narrowed by deposits of cholesterol and cell waste, a process called atherosclerosis. If allowed to build up over time, this blocks the blood supply to the heart, and hence the oxygen supply, and this causes a heart attack. Medical science has allowed many more people to survive severe heart attacks than used to, but the remaining heart tissue after such an attack may be damaged, and this may lead to heart failure. Professor Peter Weissberg, Medical Director of the British Heart Foundation, told us that heart failure is now a rapidly growing problem in the elderly (Q 275).

4.17. Treatment of heart attack through the use of "clot-busting" drugs has been effective, though it has taken many years for the UK to have developed systems to implement such evidence-based procedures. Professor Weissberg saw the reason for the delay being because of up-front costs: the NHS being concerned with annual budgets rather than the large future savings that may result from the provision of a treatment (QQ 284-285). He saw that applying best practice quickly and efficiently was essential to preventing morbidity in the elderly.

4.18. Professor Weissberg added that a major focus of research should be on repairing the organs affected by vascular disease using stem cells (Q 275). Studying embryonic stem cells would help improve understanding of the molecular mechanisms and molecular biology of tissue differentiation. This might allow the development of treatments "to start tripping the switches by

---

[71] Lowin et al, *Alzheimer's disease in the UK: comparative evidence on cost of illness and volume of health services research funding*, International Journal of Geriatric Psychiatry (2001) vol 16, pp 1143 – 1148.

[72] Final Report of the Review by Derek Wanless, *Securing Our Future Health: Taking A Long-Term View*, April 2002.

pharmacological means to induce a mature heart cell to start dividing again, which it would not normally do". (Q 300)

Cancer

4.19. Although cancer is a significant cause of death at all ages, absolute mortality rates from cancer increase sharply with age. According to Cancer Research UK, over 140,000 people over 70 are diagnosed with cancer every year, amounting to 52% of all cancers diagnosed in the UK; and over 100,000 people over 70 die of cancer every year. In this age range the most common are lung, prostate, breast and colorectal cancers. Survival rates from lung and breast cancer are particularly strongly age-related, diminishing greatly in the over 70 age group. Survival rates for prostate and colorectal cancers begin to diminish markedly only past the age of 80.[73]

4.20. Cancer is not necessarily more aggressive in older people, but there is evidence showing that a delay in diagnosis is more severe. Professor Robert Souhami, Director of Policy and Communication at Cancer Research UK, saw the need for sociological research to disentangle the factors affecting cancer diagnosis and treatment in older people (Q 513).

4.21. Whilst expenditure on cancer research is largest by far of all diseases in the UK, it tends not to be specifically targeted at cancers affecting older people. Professor Souhami told us that "If you were to look at the generality of funding in cancer and say, 'How much of that is specifically devoted towards therapeutic and other aspects of cancer as it affects an elderly population?' the answer is a very small proportion" (Q 489), contrasting this with the position in the United States, where more emphasis is given to older people. He also pointed to a gap in research relating DNA damage and cancer: "The issues of whether or not there is a decreased efficiency in repairing DNA damage... as you get older are very under-funded in the UK" (Q 496).

4.22. It is understandable that research tends to be targeted at younger age-groups, since they (and their families) may be thought to have more to gain from early diagnosis and cure. We do not in any way question the importance of such research, nor do we suggest any decrease in the amount spent on it. But Professor Souhami agreed that "Cancer Research UK and its partners do not invest enough specifically into the questions of cancer as it affects an ageing population" (Q 489). Moreover, if the current incidence of cancer is unchanged, the ageing population will result by 2025 in an extra 100,000 cases being diagnosed annually, and the vast majority of these cases will be in the over 70s.[74] If only for this reason, we believe that this country should follow the lead of the United States and Europe, and emphasise the position of older people.

4.23. **We recommend that the Government and research councils should, when allocating money to cancer research, place more emphasis on those cancers particularly prevalent among the elderly. We encourage Cancer Research UK and other charities to do likewise.**

---

[73] Cancer Research UK, p 304.

[74] Cancer Research UK, p 305.

The musculoskeletal system

4.24. Musculoskeletal disorders include problems with bones, joints and musculature, all of which undergo some progressive deterioration with age. They also include rheumatic diseases, which cover arthritis (inflammation of joints) and rheumatism (more general aches and pains in bones, muscles and joints). About 5 million people in the UK suffer from osteoarthritis, which results from the cartilage protecting joints wearing away, thus affecting older people disproportionately. Osteoporosis describes a condition of reduced bone density, leading to increased susceptibility to fractures. It is most common in the over 50s—one in three women, and one in twelve men, go on to develop it.

4.25. Professor Cooper described the burden of musculoskeletal disorders: "the prevalence of musculoskeletal disorders in all adults is 25%, the second most frequent cause of medical consultation after psychiatric disorder, and 25% of the total costs of illness in Europe ... Seven million adults in the UK have arthritis with long-term health problems; two million people visit their GP every year with osteoarthritis; and 4.4 million people have X-ray evidence of osteoarthritis" (Q 47).

4.26. Professor Graham Russell, Norman Collisson Professor of Musculoskeletal Science, Oxford University, told us in evidence that there was a genetic basis underlying most musculoskeletal disorders, particularly osteoarthritis, rheumatoid arthritis, many of the other forms of arthritis, and osteoporosis, but that most of these were not single gene disorders, but more complex genetic disorders with many factors contributing (Q 44).

4.27. One of the consequences of musculoskeletal deterioration is an increased vulnerability of older people to falling. Because muscles lose their strength and bones their ability to heal, falls often lead to bone fracture, which can result in permanent immobility.[75] Professor Rose Anne Kenny, Head of the Falls and Syncope Unit, University of Newcastle, told us:

"In the UK, 30% of those over 65 will fall at least once a year, and 40% of those over 75 will fall at least twice a year. Falls are the commonest reason cited for admission to institutional care, and for 40% of admissions to nursing homes or residential homes in the UK the top reason cited is falls." (Q 353)

4.28. However, there was some good news in terms of hip fracture, a common consequence of falling among older people:

"The mortality rates are improving with hip fracture. I am focusing on hip fracture because that is the expensive one and the one with the heaviest consequences. It is 20% one year mortality now whereas it was about 35% ten years ago. So mortality rates from hip fracture surgery are improving." (Q 354)

4.29. The decrease in muscle mass and reduced functional capacity of muscle is an important contributor to the reduced quality of life, and loss of independence, among older people. A recent study at the Royal Free Hospital which looked at muscle strength in males and females between 70 and 75 found that 50% of females and 15% of males were unable to mount a 30 cm step without holding on to a handrail. It also found that 80% of

---

[75] Biosciences Federation, p 330.

females and half of men between 70 and 75 were not able to walk at a pace of three miles per hour, and that 80% of females and half of the men had limitation of their shoulder movement such that they could not comfortably wash their hair (Q 353). We have already stressed the importance of exercise at any age in the prevention of muscle loss.[76]

Parkinson's Disease

4.30. At any one time, over 100,000 people in the UK have Parkinson's disease, and the great majority of these are older people. The disease affects one person in every thousand of the population, but for the over 70s this rises to one in fifty; the disease is one of the most common neurological conditions affecting older people. For reasons as yet unknown, it affects Caucasian people more than those of Asian or African origin, and the symptoms also tend to be different: Caucasian people are more likely to complain of tremor, while those of Afro-Caribbean origin describe stiffness as the main problem.

4.31. It is the degeneration of a specific area of the brain which results in the reduction of dopamine, the chemical messenger responsible for the efficient working of the motor coordination centres of the brain. Some loss of dopamine is a normal consequence of the ageing process, but in people with Parkinson's around 80% of dopamine has been lost by the time the disease produces the physical signs associated with it: tremor, slowness, stiffness and speech problems. The cause of this loss of dopamine is unclear, and there is no known cure, although the symptoms can be alleviated by drugs which replace dopamine or mimic its actions.

4.32. Although the physical consequences of Parkinson's are well known, it is not so widely known that between 20% and 30% of people with Parkinson's will suffer from dementia (Q 304).[77]

Dementia

4.33. "Dementia" describes symptoms which include memory loss, confusion, and problems with speech and understanding. These are caused by a deterioration of brain function. The deterioration is most commonly caused by the onset of Alzheimer's disease, which progressively kills off brain cells and is characterised by particular pathological markers in brain tissue. However dementia may also be of the "vascular" type, where the damage is linked to impaired blood flow (and which may also be linked to a stroke), or of the "Lewy body" type—Lewy bodies being the pathological markers that are also associated with Parkinson's disease. Indeed, the major difference between Dementia with Lewy Bodies (DLB) and Parkinson's disease appears to be the region of brain tissue that is affected (Q 307).[78]

4.34. In written evidence, the Alzheimer's Society explained that "dementia is not a natural part of ageing, but age is the most significant known risk factor, and that over the age of 65 "the risk of dementia doubles every five years".[79] Some studies have shown that people with a high blood pressure in middle

---

[76] Paragraphs 3.21 to 3.26.

[77] From the evidence of Mrs Linda Kelly, p 164.

[78] From the evidence of Professor Clive Ballard, p 165.

[79] p 159.

age have an increased risk of developing dementia. Apart from early-onset Alzheimer's, it does not appear to be a hereditary condition.

4.35. There is as yet no known cure for dementia. Some treatments have been developed, some of which appear to slow the progress of disease, but in general their clinical and cost effectiveness has not yet been clearly demonstrated. For example, an innovative technique to immunise against the formation of amyloid deposits in brain, which showed promise in animal experiments, caused adverse effects in humans, which have yet to be circumvented in order to allow the efficacy of such an approach to be properly assessed. Professor Carol Brayne, Professor of Public Health Medicine, Cambridge University, told us that "most of the biological lab-based stuff is aimed at providing the bullet cure, and given the mixture of pathologies that we see in the older age groups, I think it is very unlikely that that is going to make an impact on old age dementia, certainly in the near future and maybe in the longer-term". (Q 312)

4.36. Alzheimer Scotland funded a review of economic costs of diseases and the expenditure on research, which was published in a peer-reviewed journal.[80] They found that the direct cost of Alzheimer's was between £7 billion and £14 billion a year, several times that of stroke, heart disease or cancer. However, research expenditure on Alzheimer's disease was 57% of that on stroke, 10% of that on heart disease and 3% of that on cancer.

Diabetes

4.37. Glucose from food is absorbed into the blood after digestion. Normally, insulin from the pancreas will regulate the amount of glucose converted by the body into energy. In someone with diabetes the body is unable to metabolise the glucose in the bloodstream, to varying degrees. Three-quarters of people with diabetes have type 2 (where the body produces either insufficient or ineffective insulin), and age is a significant risk factor in developing it. It usually occurs in those over 40, though those from a black or ethnic minority group are at increased risk from age 25. Obesity is also a risk factor for type 2 diabetes. Early diagnosis of diabetes is essential; otherwise it may lead to complications, including blindness. People with diabetes are at increased risk from other health problems, including cardiovascular diseases and stroke.

4.38. There are links between the causes of type 2 diabetes and dementia. Amyloid plaques—fibrous deposits of protein—have been seen in the pancreas of some diabetics and may stop production of insulin. It is also suspected that amyloid plaques can build up in the brain and kill off cells, leading to Alzheimer's disease. Dr Frans van der Ouderaa told us: "the etiological factors for dementia go from overweight and metabolic dysregulation to diabetes to cardiovascular disease to dementia. If you do not become overweight, if you do not get diabetes, then the risk of dementia is maybe 10% of the risk of you getting it [otherwise]" (Q 123).

4.39. The Medical Research Council is funding research into amyloid diseases. A team at the National Amyloidosis Centre in London, through MRC funding, have developed a drug that destabilises amyloid deposits, allowing them to be

---

[80] Lowin et al, *Alzheimer's disease in the UK: comparative evidence on cost of illness and volume of health services research funding*, International Journal of Geriatric Psychiatry (2001) vol 16, pp 1143 – 1148.

broken down. The new drug offers a new approach to treating a range of amyloid diseases.[81]

Sensory impairments

Sight

4.40. There are in the UK between four and a quarter and four and a half million people with significant loss of vision through macular degeneration. Some 70% of these are over 65 (Q 347).[82] Other common causes of sight loss are cataracts and glaucoma. A study funded by the Thomas Pocklington Trust found that one in 8 people over 75, and one in 3 people over 90, suffer from severe sight loss.[83] Older women are more likely than men to suffer from sight loss, even after adjusting for age differences.

4.41. Sight loss is often regarded, particularly by those who suffer from it, as an automatic consequence of ageing about which nothing can be done. There is "a singular lack of reliable social research on sight loss,"[84] but it seems that a frequent reaction from older people is that sight loss means "I cannot see and therefore I cannot do"—this despite the fact that there is often an amazing level of ability left which is untapped, unused and un-nurtured (Q 347).[85]

Hearing

4.42. Professor Karen Steel of the Wellcome Trust Sanger Institute told us that in the UK there are approximately nine million people who have a significant hearing impairment in one ear or the other. Hearing loss is the commonest of the sensory impairments suffered in old age, and is experienced by half of people over 60. Yet, even more than sight loss, it "has long been regarded as an inevitable consequence of growing old, not only among the medical profession but also by the man in the street, and so very often people do not complain about it as much as they should as they are getting older". Social withdrawal is for many people the main tactic deliberately used to avoid embarrassment. There is a stigma attached to hearing impairment which is present to a markedly lesser degree, if indeed at all, in the case of sight impairment; glasses can be regarded as fashion accessories, but the same is not true of hearing aids (Q 351, QQ 361-362). The scale of the problem means that it should be a priority for research, yet the opposite seems to be the case.

4.43. Professor Steel added:

"We know virtually nothing about the causes of hearing impairment as people get older. We know nothing at a molecular level and practically nothing at a cellular level but we do know some things that are important. For example, there are three independent studies now that have demonstrated that age-related hearing impairment has heritability of about 50%. What that means is that about half of the hearing impairment is

---

[81] Research Councils UK, p 198.

[82] From the evidence of Mr Mike Brace, Chief Executive, Vision 2020, p 178.

[83] JR Evans et al, *Prevalence of visual impairment in people aged 75 years and older in Britain*, British Journal of Ophthalmology 2002;86:795-800 cited in p 408.

[84] Thomas Pocklington Trust, p 408.

[85] From the evidence of Mr Mike Brace , p 178.

something to do with the variants of the genes we carry and the remaining half is probably due to environmental factors. Noise is almost inevitably going to be one of those, but we should not forget drugs, we should not forget infections as well because these can also affect hearing, and I suspect that diet may have an effect. So we actually know very little." (Q 349)

4.44. One thing however which is perfectly clear is the damage to our hearing caused by excess noise, and that damage is irreversible. "Damage to our hearing is a one-way process because we are born with a set of sensory cells within our inner ear that are not replaced when they die, and any noise damage or any other sort of damage that damages them and makes those cells die leads to irreparable longer term damage. It is a one-way process basically and we never regenerate these sensory hair cells. The level of sound is obviously very important and the length of time of exposure is very important." (Q 348)

4.45. We asked whether there was evidence that using Walkmans, iPods and other personal amplification systems caused damage to hearing. We were told that at present there is only limited evidence of this, but that this is probably because most such systems are used by young people whose hearing is fairly robust, so that some small amount of physical damage within the ear would not be noticed yet (Q 348). We believe that this is an important topic for research. If evidence does show that the use of such sound systems is going to cause people to lose their hearing ability later on in life, now is the time for the research to be done, so that appropriate precautions may be taken.

4.46. About 4 million people would probably benefit from using a hearing aid, but only 1.5 million people have one, and it is estimated that half of them find their hearing aids inadequate and do not use them. One of the main challenges is to produce hearing aids which give better frequency resolution and better temporal resolution. We believe that the profits to be made by any company which can produce a markedly improved hearing aid must be very substantial. Yet this is a challenge which industry seems reluctant to take up. We consider this in Chapter 6.

Touch

4.47. The only evidence we received on touch was from Dr R. Conrad, formerly Assistant Director of the MRC's Applied Psychology Unit at Cambridge.[86] He explained the importance to an older person of cutaneous sensation ("Is my finger actually in contact with a surface? Have I actually swallowed the small pill?"). The same was true for proprioception, the exact knowledge of where one's limbs, especially fingers, were in space ("Is my finger solely on the correct button? Have I pressed the button hard enough?"). Yet little was known about this, and whereas there was a great deal of quantitative data available relating to sight and hearing impairment, this was seriously lacking for other sensory systems. In his view there was an urgent need for epidemiological studies to establish the capabilities of older people in different age groups.

---

[86] p 355.

The cost of sensory impairment

4.48. Leaving aside the loss of faculties caused by sensory impairment, social withdrawal, and the psychological impacts that follow from these, there are direct financial costs. A study in the United States in 1998 suggested that onset of hearing loss to a person in their seventies cost something of the order of $43,000 in hearing aid provision and loss of income. We did not receive comparable figures for sight loss, but it is plain that any intervention that can help reduce those costs, for example by picking up the hearing or sight loss at an earlier stage, will be a benefit accruing not only to the individual but also to society (Q 372).[87]

Oral deterioration

4.49. Deterioration of oral health is particularly significant for the effect it has on quality of life, not just directly, but also in many other ways. A person's oral health status can affect not just how they chew, taste and enjoy food, but can have more profound physical and psychological influences on how they enjoy life: how they look, how they speak, and how they socialise, as well as their self-esteem, self image and feelings of social well-being.[88] But although oral ill-health has such a profound effect on the psycho-social welfare—particularly of the elderly who have poor oral health—it tends to be a poor relation in terms of the notice the public take of it, and in terms of the research funding it attracts (Q 96).[89]

4.50. The current shortage of dentists is well-known. We know that the Government is addressing this problem although, given the time needed for training new dentists, this will be a slow process unless more qualified dentists can be encouraged to work in this country. This shortage is however a matter of particular concern in relation to older people, since they need more frequent access to dentists, but are less able to join the queues of people attempting to register with new dentists.

4.51. **We recommend that the Department of Health should continue to take urgent steps to remedy the shortage of dentists, and to encourage a habit of more frequent check-ups, especially among older people.**

Conclusion

4.52. **Older people are disproportionately affected by many specific diseases and sensory impairments, and the expenditure directed at these diseases appears to be far lower than would be expected. A population with a growing number of older people will result in an increasing burden on society from some conditions for which age is a significant risk factor.**

4.53. **The Government should re-examine their research priorities, and promote expenditure on research into the alleviation of those conditions which disproportionately affect older people.**

---

[87] From the evidence of Professor Karen Steel, p 186.

[88] Professor Aubrey Sheiham and Dr Georgios Tsakos, p 395.

[89] From the evidence of Professor Elizabeth Kay, p 41.

CHAPTER 5: THE ENVIRONMENTAL CHALLENGE AND ASSISTIVE TECHNOLOGY

Introduction

5.1. We saw in Chapter 3 that the ageing process is malleable, and that non-genetic factors can have an important impact on how people age and how long they live. Environment can have powerful enabling or disabling impacts on older age. In particular, unsupportive environments (poor transport, poor housing, higher levels of crime, etc) discourage active lifestyle and social participation. Inactivity and isolation accelerate physical and psychological declines, creating a negative spiral towards premature, preventable ill health and dependency. Indeed, disability can be defined not as a physical state that exists without reference to other factors but as a mismatch between what a person can do and what their environment requires of them.

5.2. Changing the environment, for example by providing assistive devices to overcome physical limitations, can effectively remove or at least postpone functional disability. A person with severe short sight would have been significantly disabled among our stone-age ancestors; the same person with spectacles today is not counted as disabled at all. During our inquiry we heard much about the nature and extent of the environmental challenge and about research being done to overcome this challenge.

The built environment

5.3. If older people need to leave their homes because they are no longer able to look after themselves, they usually do so only with great reluctance. If they wish to stay in their homes for so long as they are fit to do so, we must ensure that their homes are fit for them to continue to live in.

5.4. The English House Condition Survey 2001 defines a "decent home" as one that meets all of the following criteria:

- it is above the current statutory minimum standard for housing;
- it is in a reasonable state of repair;
- it has reasonably modern facilities and services; and
- it provides a reasonable degree of thermal comfort.

In 1996, nearly half (48%) of people aged 60 or over lived in a home that did not meet these standards.[90] By the time of the 2001 survey this figure had fallen to 34%. This is a considerable and welcome improvement, but it is nevertheless a matter for concern that one third of older people were then living in housing that did not meet these minimum criteria.

5.5. In the case of older people, thermal comfort is particularly important. Help the Aged estimate that every year the mortality rate amongst older people in England and Wales rises during the months from December to March by between 20,000 and 50,000 extra deaths from illnesses caused or exacerbated by exposure to the cold. The ONS state that in England and Wales in 2004, 21,500 people over the age of 65 died as a direct result of the

---

[90] English House Condition Survey 1996.

cold.[91] Older people tend to live in the oldest houses which have poor insulation and are hardest to heat. Cold and damp aggravate circulatory diseases, and this can in turn lead to strokes and heart attacks, or to respiratory diseases and pneumonia.

5.6. This is a major problem for this country. The table below shows that in October 2003, of the countries then members of the European Union, other than the Mediterranean countries and Sweden, only Ireland had a worse record:

TABLE 5

Excess winter mortality as % increase over non-winter deaths[92]

Ireland	19%
United Kingdom	18%
Austria	14%
Belgium	13%
France	13%
Luxembourg	12%
Denmark	12%
Germany	11%
Netherlands	11%
Finland	10%

The excess winter mortality rate is the figure which compares the total number of deaths during the period December–March with the average number of deaths in the preceding and following four-month periods.

In Germany and Finland, which have much severer winters than we do, the levels of cold-related mortality are little over half the levels in the UK.

5.7. The Warm Homes and Energy Conservation Act 2000 requires the Government to develop and publish a strategy for ensuring that, so far as possible, people do not live in fuel poverty.[93] The UK Fuel Poverty Strategy was made under that Act. The first Annual Progress Report found that in March 2003 older people made up around half of the estimated three million fuel poor households. From an analysis carried out by the Department of Trade and Industry (DTI), it appears that in England in 2001 7.6% of pensioner couple households and 22.2% of single pensioner households were in fuel poverty. This compares with 8.4% of all households.[94] It can be

---

[91] Help the Aged Campaigns and News, 2005

[92] Dr John D. Healy, Research Fellow, University College Dublin, *Excess winter mortality in Europe: a cross country analysis, identifying key risk factors*, Journal of Epidemiology & Community Health, October 2003.

[93] For the purposes of this Act, a person is regarded as living "in fuel poverty" if he is a member of a household living on a lower income in a home which cannot be kept warm at reasonable cost. The most widely accepted definition of a fuel poor household is one which needs to spend more than 10% of its income to heat its home to an adequate standard of warmth. This is generally defined as 21°C in the living room and 18°C in the other occupied rooms – the temperatures recommended by the World Health Organisation.

[94] p 63.

argued that some at least of older people living in fuel poverty could afford to heat their homes better, but choose instead to spend their money on other things, not knowing (or in some cases perhaps not caring) that they are more vulnerable to cold than younger people. But we think it likely that the majority of those who live in fuel poverty do so because they have no alternative.

5.8. The Government's target is the elimination of fuel poverty in vulnerable households in England by 2010.[95] This is also the target of the Northern Ireland Department for Social Development. The corresponding target of the Welsh Assembly is 2012. The Scottish Executive is committed to a 30% reduction in fuel poverty by 2006, and total elimination by 2016.[96]

5.9. The Fuel Poverty Advisory Group, a non-departmental public body, was set up to monitor the progress of the Government's Fuel Poverty Strategy. In its 2004 Annual Report, the Group said that it believed the Government could achieve their target of eradicating fuel poverty in vulnerable households in England by 2010, but that this would not be achieved by "business as usual". It added that the DoH and the NHS had been "particularly unresponsive to [its] modest request for assistance in getting energy efficiency help to those most in need", and expressed astonishment that the Office of the Deputy Prime Minister (ODPM), with its responsibilities for housing, did not focus more on fuel poverty issues. In its latest Annual Report, published in March 2005, the Group continues to criticise departments, other than the Department for the Environment, Food and Rural Affairs (Defra) and DTI, for their lack of involvement, and states: "It is essential now—with only about five years remaining to meet the 2010 target—that the Government faces up to the difficult areas... and provides action plans for dealing with fuel poverty in these areas".[97]

5.10. Given that, as we have said, older people make up around half of the households at risk, we concur in this view. The problem is to some extent caused by the age of some of the housing stock, with poor insulation leading to fuel inefficiency. We accept that this problem is therefore not susceptible of a quick solution. We believe however that a "target" which may or may not be met is not appropriate for a problem whose cost each year is measured in the lives of many thousands of older people.

5.11. **The Office of the Deputy Prime Minister and the Department of Health should join with the Department for the Environment, Food and Rural Affairs and the Department of Trade and Industry in pressing ahead with the preparation of detailed plans for the elimination of deaths of older people caused by cold and damp, and should provide the resources to implement these plans.**

---

[95] *Fuel Poverty in England: The Government's Plan for Action*, November 2004.

[96] *UK Fuel Poverty Strategy* 2nd Annual Progress Report, 2004

[97] In our contemporaneous report on *Energy Efficiency* (House of Lords Select Committee on Science and Technology, 2nd Report (2005-06) HL Paper 21-I), we refer to the "lifeline" tariffs introduced in many American states after the oil crises of the 1970s. These tariffs provide for cheap electricity sufficient to meet the most basic needs (typically up to around 50-60% of average household consumption), and more expensive electricity at higher levels of use. This approach ensures that electricity for basic necessities is affordable.

Lifetime homes

5.12. The average age of those using housing in this country is continuing to increase. Much could be done to improve the quality of life of older people if buildings were from the outset designed in the knowledge that they would probably one day be lived in by older people.

5.13. In evidence given to the House of Commons Select Committee on the Office of the Deputy Prime Minister on 10 March 2004, Phil Hope MP, the Minister then responsible for the Building Regulations, announced that he had asked the Building Regulations Advisory Committee to review Part M of the Building Regulations to see whether it would be practicable to incorporate into it the Lifetime Homes Standard. It was, he said, "one of our continuing commitments to encourage better design and to build inclusive communities with improved quality of life for all". On the same date, ODPM issued a press notice explaining that the purpose of the review would be to look at changes to the Regulations which "would allow people to remain in their own homes for longer as they age[d] or their circumstances change[d]". It would be examining such features as having stairs designed to be able to accommodate a chair lift at a later stage; ground floor bedrooms and WCs; and ground floor space for the installation of showers.

5.14. While the announcement of this review was a welcome development, we note that it came as long as five years after the Joseph Rowntree Report on Part M and Lifetime Home Standards, which ODPM had accepted. However at the date of this report, nearly 18 months later, the review has barely got under way. The press notice issued in March 2004 stated that "the new standards could be in place in two years' time". This appears no longer to be the target; in March 2005 it was stated[98] that the review was undertaken "with a view to legislating by 2007". Once the new standards eventually are in place, compliance with them will need to be closely monitored. But even then, as Professor Anthea Tinker pointed out to us, any change in the Building Regulations is not going to help most older people because they are in existing homes (Q 241). The amended Regulations will be of little benefit to older people for many years.

5.15. **We urge the Government to take forward urgently the review of Part M of the Building Regulations, to bring up to date the Lifetime Home Standards, and to amend the Regulations to incorporate the revised standards.**

5.16. The Welsh Assembly have adopted the Lifetime Home Standards for the housing for which they are responsible, and some housing corporations have voluntarily done so. Until the Building Regulations are amended, ODPM should encourage all those responsible for social housing to do likewise. If necessary, this should be made a condition for the release of funds.

Older drivers

5.17. The Driver and Vehicle Licensing Authority (DVLA) have records of 38 million drivers, 2.5 million of whom are over 70. In 2002 68% of men aged over 70 were driving licence holders—an increase over the 59% who held a licence a decade ago. In the same period the percentage of women aged over 70 holding driving licences increased from 17% to 28%.

---

98 *Opportunity Age,* Cm 6466 , paragraph 3.19.

Projections from the Department for Transport (DfT) suggest that by the years 2020 to 2025, 78% of men and 58% of women over 70 will be licence holders.[99] The Department for Transport is keen for older people to stay driving as long as they possibly can (Q 167). We agree that this is very desirable.

5.18. At present section 99 of the Road Traffic Act 1988 provides for the automatic expiry of driving licences at age 70, and requires drivers who reach that age to make an application for their licence to be renewed. When the age limit of 70 was set in 1975, only 15% of those above this age were drivers; the figure now is 45%, and over 18,000 licence-holders are now aged 90 or over. Some of this change is due to the increase in LE, but mainly it comes about because the generation which almost automatically learned to drive and was able to afford cars is now reaching the 70 deadline. In its written evidence the Department conceded that this choice of age was "somewhat arbitrary". We agree.

5.19. The Department told us that in spite of the decline in function associated with normal ageing; research internationally (including in the UK) showed little increase in the incidence of road traffic accidents with advancing age. Where such accidents do happen, they tend to occur where older drivers are turning at junctions. But the increased frailty of the older population means that accidents involving older drivers disproportionately result in fatal or serious injuries.

5.20. The view of Professor Desmond O'Neill from the Department of Clinical Gerontology at Trinity College Dublin was that:

"All the crash data suggests that older drivers are the safest drivers, and this is largely accounted for by strategic decisions on driving, limiting driving at night, for example, and in bad weather, and avoiding complex traffic situations, and by withdrawing prematurely from driving ... for the moment self-regulation seems to be effective, certainly from a public health/safety point of view" (Q 358).

5.21. Professor O'Neill pointed us to two studies suggesting that there are no safety-related reasons for age-related medical screening. The first such study compared the position in Finland with that in Sweden.[100] In Sweden there is no age-related screening, medical or otherwise; the right to drive is given for life. Finland by contrast in 1996 had strict medical screening from age 45. Despite this, the study showed that this did not lead to better safety for older car drivers and occupants than in Sweden. Similarly, a more recent study of older drivers in the Australian States found evidence that in Victoria, where there is no age-based assessment, older drivers "may have a significantly safer record regarding overall involvement in serious casualty crashes" than in other States (such as New South Wales) which have stringent requirements for both health and on-road assessment.[101]

5.22. We were told by Charlotte Atkins MP, then a Parliamentary Under-Secretary of State at the DfT, that the DVLA has commissioned an independent

---

[99] p 57.

[100] Hakamies-Blomkvist et al, *Medical Screening of Older Drivers as a Traffic Safety Measure – A Comparative Finnish-Swedish Evaluation Study*, Journal of the American Geriatrics Society 1996, vol 44.

[101] Langford et al, *Some Consequences of Different Older Driver Licensing Procedures in Australia*, Accident Analysis & Prevention 36 (2004).

review which hopes to report by October this year, examining whether the age for licence renewal should be raised from 70 to 75, or whether any other age (or perhaps no other specific age) would be appropriate for licences automatically to be renewed. She thought that "a limit at 75 plus would be worth keeping ... having an age—75, 70, whatever—when people have to consider the issues and make a judgment is quite useful" (Q 557).

5.23. **We recommend that, when reaching decisions on the review commissioned by the DVLA, the Department for Transport should not exclude the option of allowing licence-holders to determine for themselves the age at which they should cease to drive.**

5.24. The problems older people have with driving are not all associated with the ability to drive. Ms Ann Frye, Head of the Mobility and Exclusion Unit at the DfT, told us that "Often it is getting in and out of the car that is the bigger problem for older people rather than actually driving it, and the way that cars are designed can make it quite difficult. Climbing over the sill which has been built in for accident protection actually can form quite a barrier. Getting the car manufacturers again to recognise the demographics and look at the buying power of more and more older people who do want to go on buying new cars is, I think, beginning to come through in the developments that we are seeing" (Q 174). Ms Yvonne Brown told us that the Mobility and Exclusion Unit had a research programme looking at modifications for vehicles which could make driving easier for older people with impairment.

5.25. The reluctance of car manufacturers to recognise these difficulties, and the benefits to be derived from overcoming them, is part of a more general problem which we consider in Chapter 6.

Mobility and public transport

5.26. There remains a large proportion of older people who are unable or unwilling to drive at all, or who are unwilling to drive on particular journeys or in particular conditions. For them, public transport is all-important. We are living with the legacy of generations where hospitals and shopping centres were built out of town. Public transport is vital for essential journeys to doctors, hospitals and shops; but it is just as vital for those journeys which allow people to remain in touch with their families and friends, and to engage fully with the wider community.

5.27. A number of witnesses told us that, while the availability of public transport, and its suitability for their particular circumstances, is a major concern for all older people, it may be less of a problem for those who have always relied on public transport. Conversely, it is a particular problem for those who have recently been obliged to stop driving. The Department for Transport told us that older people who had never been drivers were much more mobile in old age than those who had had to give up driving, and that one major cause was lack of familiarity with how public transport worked.[102] Professor O'Neill said that a number of studies showed that older people who have retired from driving are more prone to depression and feel socially isolated (Q 365).

5.28. Ms Frye explained that there was a very clear correlation between age and disability, since two-thirds of disabled people were over pensionable age. One of the Department's main policy planks was implementing the transport

---

[102] p 59.

provisions of the Disability Discrimination Act 1996, progressively requiring not just wheelchair access to buses and trains but also very simple, practical things like colour contrast, non-slip surfaces, better hand-holds, bell-pushes which one could ring before getting to one's feet and lose one's balance. All these, she said, would have a huge impact on the ability of older people to travel (Q 167). This is welcome, but Professor Robert Weale from the Institute of Gerontology at King's College London gave us examples of further changes which could make transport facilities even more user-friendly. These included the legibility of instructions by attention to the shapes of letters, their contrast and their positions, and the avoidance of blue and violet colour combinations. Boarding steps for aircraft were now in his view an anachronism.

5.29. In addition to fears about the suitability and ease of access of public transport systems, we believe that many older people are inhibited from using them because of concerns about unforeseen events. All too often train seat reservations are omitted because of operational difficulties, a platform is changed at the last moment, train toilets are out of order necessitating a walk through multiple carriages, buses fail to appear, and so on. The assistance provided to older people in these circumstances is often limited or non-existent.

5.30. We do not for a moment wish to play down the importance of increasing the mobility of disabled people. But "the Disability Discrimination Act tends to focus on young disabled people."[103] Although two thirds of disabled people are over pensionable age, the great majority of older people are not disabled, and it is their concerns which we particularly have in mind.

5.31. In a speech to the Community Transport Association on 15 May 2003 discussing a report of the Social Exclusion Unit (SEU), Barbara Roche, then the Minister for Social Exclusion, said that over a year 1.4 million people miss, turn down or choose not to seek medical help because of transport problems. Although we have been given no figures, it is a fair assumption that a high proportion of those 1.4 million are older people. Missed doctor and hospital appointments mean poorer health, and that in turn means more costs to the NHS. But transport comes from one budget, health from another. Ms Frye told us that the DfT was discussing the findings of the SEU report with other departments, including the DoH (Q 167). We hope that these discussions will bear in mind that every pound spent on improved transport which allows older people to attend medical appointments they might otherwise have missed may well be a pound—or more—saved by the NHS.

5.32. In oral evidence Ms Atkins was asked about the involvement of her Department in the planning of the new housing developments in the South-East announced by the Deputy Prime Minister. She assured us that the two departments were closely cooperating over the transport needs of these developments, but was unable to confirm that these plans took particular account of the special needs of older people (QQ 558-560). We regard this as unsatisfactory, given that older people are a growing fraction of the population who are particularly reliant on public transport.

---

[103] Professor Alan Newell, Queen Mother Research Centre for Information Technology to support Older People, University of Dundee, p 369.

5.33. **We believe the evidence clearly shows how older people enter into a negative spiral towards dependency through social isolation and inactivity, often founded on lack of access to suitable transport, amenities and opportunities for exercise.**

5.34. **Government, local authorities, transport companies and service providers should plan on the assumption that the average age of users and the proportion of older users will continue to increase. Compliance with regulations requiring provision for older people should be monitored.**

Communication

5.35. One of the biggest transformations to take place in our society over the last ten or twenty years has been the explosive growth in communication technology. Although such a transformation has the potential to improve the lives of older people greatly, the older age groups have in fact benefited the least. Emails are increasingly taking over from letter-writing as a means of personal communication, and mobile phones from telephone landlines. Consumer information about products and services is in many instances provided primarily through internet websites. Many companies now operate highly automated telephone switchboards, which require familiarity with speaking to a machine and a capacity to listen carefully and make rapid decisions from lists of offered options which may be presented using unfamiliar terminology.

5.36. Professor Newell told us:

"Information technology appears to have made an enormous impact on every aspect of society in the developed world. A more detailed examination of statistics, however, indicates that some groups are not benefiting from these advances. This situation has been referred to as the Digital Divide—the divide between those groups of people who benefit from information technology and those who do not or cannot access it ... Much current information technology appears to have been designed by and for young men who are besotted by technology, and are more interested in playing with it, and exploring what the software can do, rather than achieving a particular goal ... Many older people and people and people with disabilities, however, lack the visual acuity, manual dexterity, and cognitive ability successfully to operate much modern technology. Many find the Windows environment, and the software associated with it, very confusing and difficult or impossible to use. Most mobile telephones require good vision and a high level of dexterity and video tape recorders are well known for providing many usability problems for older people ... Many people have developed very low expectations of older and disabled people's interest in and ability to use information technology products. A major cause of this, however, is government's and industry's lack of sensitivity to the particular needs and wants of older people and hence the inappropriate nature and poor usability of most products for older people. In general, the problem is not that older people are unwilling to use 'new technology'. The problem is that they are overwhelmed and frightened by the manifestations of technology which have been designed by people who do not understand the needs and abilities of older people."[104]

---

104 p 367.

Professor Newell also pointed out that older people are major users of government and e-health services, and was critical of the Government's "lack of sensitivity" to the needs of older people.

5.37. In December 2000 the Ageing Panel of the DTI's Foresight programme reported to the Government on Communications and Information Technology.[105] They commented that "ICT is at the centre of social change" and that it included:

- internet shopping;

- education;

- health care;

- access to information;

- personal contacts and communications;

- public services;

- transport;

- local and national government; and

- democratic processes.

The report stated that perceptions of older people needed reviewing, that in general they were not technophobic, but that even when the ICT generation becomes old there will still be challenges of poorer eyesight, memory etc. They recommended that "there should be mandatory inclusivity during periods of rapid technological development (e.g. e-commerce)" and that "Government has a role to play as a promoter and exemplar of good practice". But Professor Newell felt that little had changed since the date of that report.

5.38. As the report implies, the generation familiar with the benefits of electronic communication is becoming the generation of older people. It is extraordinary that Government and industry should pay so little attention to their needs. We consider the problems of industry in the next chapter. We believe that the Government should set an example by paying particular attention to the needs of older people when designing websites and planning electronic services which are intended to be used by older people.

5.39. **We believe that some of the most exciting opportunities for scientific advance to benefit older people arise through use of information technology. Industry self-regulation has notably failed to address these needs and opportunities.**

5.40. A specific matter of importance to older people is the availability of broadband. Broadband can be particularly useful in rural areas, where social isolation of older people is often most severe; and it is precisely here that broadband is often not available. In February 2004 the House of Commons Trade and Industry Committee stated: "It may be that broadband becomes so ubiquitous amongst those members of the population able to access it that those who cannot become genuinely excluded. Under such circumstances a

---

[105] The Age Shift – Priorities for Action.

Universal Service Obligation (USO) might be considered."[106] In its response, submitted in May 2004, the Office of Communications (Ofcom) agreed that it was "too early to judge whether a USO for broadband is necessary. Universal service is about ensuring the affordability and accessibility of basic communications services. Currently around 12% of UK homes subscribe to a broadband service and availability is almost 90% of the UK. On this basis, Ofcom's view is that broadband has not yet developed to the extent that it should be considered a basic service for the purposes of a USO."[107] In the year that has elapsed since that response the proportion of homes subscribing to a broadband service has considerably increased. We believe that, at least among older people, broadband has now become a basic service which should be made available.

5.41. Our attention has been drawn to a pilot project, sponsored by DfES, which began in November 2001 in the Framlingham area of Suffolk as an attempt to bridge the divide between those who did and those who did not have internet access. Some 1500 computers were made available to households meeting selection criteria, with priority being given to the socially excluded. Subsequently the project succeeded in getting broadband to five surrounding villages which did not previously have access to it. We commend the Department for sponsoring this pilot project, which we believe could serve as a model for the extension of broadband to other rural areas.

5.42. One of Ofcom's duties under the Communications Act 2003 is to have regard to the desirability of encouraging the availability and use of broadband. Ofcom should encourage and support such projects. Where service providers believe it is still not commercially viable for broadband to be made available in rural areas, in our view the time has now come for Ofcom to persuade them to make it available. Where persuasion is not enough, it should rely on its regulatory powers.

5.43. **The Government's target should be that every home, including those in rural areas where social isolation of older people is often severe, should receive access to affordable high bandwidth IT connection within 3 years. If necessary, Ofcom should rely on its regulatory powers to secure this. Local authorities should offer older people training packages in the use of IT.**

Assistive technology

5.44. "Assistive technology" (AT) is a broad generic term, defined by the Foundation for Assistive Technology, a body supported by the Department of Health, as covering "any product or service designed to enable independence for disabled and older people". Help the Aged suggest that it covers:

- Mobility aids, e.g. powered wheelchairs, stair lifts;

- Aids to daily living, e.g. accessible baths, showers or toilets;

- Environmental control systems, e.g. infra-red controls to allow the user to operate household equipment such as radios, TVs, light switches;

---

[106] Second Report from the Trade and Industry Committee, Session 2003-04, *UK Broadband Market*, HC 321.

[107] Fourth Special Report from the Trade and Industry Select Committee, Session 2003-04, *UK Broadband Market, Responses to the Committee's Second Report*, HC 596.

- Communication equipment, including accessible telephone equipment or videophones used for telemedicine;

- Security devices, e.g. community alarms to warn carers or other care services if anything is untoward;

- Smart Homes providing electronic or computer-controlled integration of assistive devices within the home;

- Beyond this, a range of more basic yet vital technologies aimed at assisting people to undertake activities of daily living. These include such aids as "jam-jar openers" and "stocking aids".

5.45. In our Call for Evidence, published in Appendix 3, we specifically asked for evidence on "the application of research in technology and design to improve the quality of life of older people, including technologies which could be used to a greater extent to benefit older people, and the development of new technologies". We are grateful for all the written and oral evidence we received. Plainly this is an area with immense potential for development. Sadly, our overall impression is that this potential is far from being realised.

5.46. We find it hard to understand the reasons for this. The problem is not new, although it is of course growing with the expanding older population. The incentive is not new: it has always been the case that people would prefer to live in their homes for as long as they safely and comfortably can. The advantages to the State are obvious: research has shown that in the United States health care costs of those with extensive AT are approximately half of those with minimal AT.[108] There is nothing remarkable about the science involved, since these are overwhelmingly applications of existing technologies to new uses. We are driven to the conclusion that this is yet another manifestation of the problem we look at more fully in the next chapter—the reluctance of industry to address a market which is ready to embrace any offer of good products at reasonable prices.

5.47. One reason for this failure of industry is "a notable absence of the meaningful involvement of older people themselves in research, particularly in technology".[109] As with IT, much AT is designed by the young with insufficient understanding of the old. "The whole of assistive technology suffers greatly from a lot of technology push and insufficient user pull." (Q 241).[110] During our visit to the University of York we saw much interesting research, but it emerged during discussion that there had as yet been little direct engagement with the intended users. We have gained the clear impression that this is currently the norm rather than an exception.

5.48. Certainly, mobility aids such as powered wheelchairs and stair lifts have been available for some time—at a price. Since we have received no evidence specifically relating to them, we content ourselves with saying that we believe there is a large market open to those who can produce imaginative designs at affordable prices. The same must be true of accessible baths, showers and toilets. Those we saw appear to be adapted from those available to able-bodied persons, rather than being designed with the assistance of those for whom they are intended.

---

[108] Professor Anthea Tinker and Ms Claudine McCreadie, p 119.

[109] Help the Aged, p 281.

[110] From the evidence of Professor Garth Johnson, Professor of Rehabilitation Engineering, University of Newcastle, p 132.

5.49. Professor Anthea Tinker explained to us what could be done:

> "One particular project was about mobility and we started by asking older people what their needs were ... and top of the list with all of them when we put them together was climbing stairs. So then we had engineering students who got together with the research team and we asked what sort of climbing aid they would want ... The researchers, the engineers and the students (because it is important that we were educating students as well about the needs of older people) went away and designed a very, very simple stair climbing aid which you could go up and down stairs with. They re-designed it in wood, took it back to the group, they tried it, they made their comments, it was then designed and it is now a prototype and it is being patented, so here is one success story." (Q 228)

It seems to us that this shows, not just what can be done, but how it should be done: by consulting the end users throughout the design process.

5.50. Professor Tinker gave us an example of how this country lags behind in this field. In the Netherlands stair lifts are installed on steep winding stairs where no one in this country would have thought of installing them. Within a few weeks of their being seen by UK housing associations and local authorities, one of those authorities had installed thirty such lifts (Q 250).

5.51. As we have said, the term "assistive technology" is used to cover almost any product designed to assist older people. Social alarms seem to us to be products which raise problems typical of those of this industry. We therefore focus on these.

5.52. One of the few British companies of any size which concentrates on the needs of older people is Tunstall Group Ltd. In their written evidence to us they describe themselves as "the world leader in Telecare", employing 750 people (mostly in the UK), 50 of these on research and development, and exporting 30% of their production. Tunstalls explained to us that the concept of social alarms had been around for over half a century, and that there were now 1.5 million people in the UK benefiting from this type of technology, monitored by 280 call centres operated by local authorities, housing corporations and some private organisations. A majority are not yet voice-based, and this puts huge pressure on the managers of the services. A second generation of alarm, now being installed, is wireless based (and so does not rely on users pressing a button). These systems are non-intrusive, they can differentiate between emergencies and false alarms, and they cover a wider range of risks (such as inactivity, or escaping gas). Third generation alarms, still being developed, will be able to predict problems and so avoid crises. By monitoring such matters as use of kitchen or bathroom, they can detect changes in the activities of the individual, and action can be taken at an early stage, avoiding more intensive and costly interventions.

5.53. The advantages of the third generation alarms are self-evident. Given that there is nothing revolutionary about the technology, we cannot understand what has prevented the development taking place years ago, and why these alarms could not already be widely in use. The problem seems to be one of scale. These are not alarms which can be sold singly to interested individuals; local authorities first have to set up the infrastructure. According to Tunstalls, national policy has been lacking, departmental responsibility confusing, and guidance to local authorities and health trusts uncoordinated.

Their answer is that "local authorities and the NHS should work closely together ... to encourage investment".[111]

5.54. Mr Sadler, the Technical Director of Tunstalls, thought that older people were naturally distrustful of any advertising that came through unfamiliar channels; they were more likely to buy his company's alarms if they were advertised through a local authority, rather than directly (Q 464). This provides a further reason for involving local authorities in this development.

5.55. We have not seen any comparison of the cost of supplying the infrastructure for such alarm systems with the savings to be made in terms of health and social care, but the United States research to which we referred in paragraph 5.43.shows that such savings may be considerable. However we can well believe that local authorities are reluctant to invest money in such projects when savings will mainly accrue to the NHS and central government. We therefore agree with Tunstalls that a national policy is essential, as is the working together of the Department of Health, the NHS, local authorities, and ODPM which is responsible for them.

5.56. Dr Stephen Ladyman MP, then a Parliamentary Under-Secretary of State at the DoH, appeared to concede as much in oral evidence to us. He said:

"We launched the Green Paper on Adult Social Care on Monday, yesterday [21 March 2005], and we made big play of the potential of assistive technology in that ... we are spending £80 million over two years, starting next year, on helping to create pilots for local authorities to try and deploy this technology ... there is a real opportunity for deploying the technology in support of older people and their carers ..."

"We [DoH] are big purchasers, and that is why we have started down this route of investing taxpayers' money in assistive technology, because if we left it to individuals to buy assistive technology and they could not afford to buy it, the result would therefore be they would have more accidents, end up in hospital, and the taxpayer would pay even more for them. So it is far better for us to make investment to prevent people becoming sick, and that is what we are intending to do. Of course we have people within the Department of Health who have an expertise in understanding the market-place and negotiating contracts with purchasers ... I have got them working on how best we can drive down the price of technologies ..." (QQ 567-596).

5.57. This is welcome news, and we are particularly glad to see formal recognition of the savings which can be achieved by expenditure on assistive technology. But we note that the spending of £80 million does not begin until next year, and that the Department is only now "starting down this route". Given that, in addition to the savings to be made, there are enormous but unquantifiable benefits for those whose accidents can be prevented, we urge the Department to hasten down this route without further delay.

5.58. **The Department of Health and the Office of the Deputy Prime Minister should make funds available to local authorities to set up the infrastructure needed for third generation social alarms. Local authorities should work closely with industry and with charities concerned with assistive technology in carrying this work forward.**

---

[111] p 98.

5.59. Dr Ladyman told us of a trip organised in October 2004 to study assistive technology in Japan (QQ 590-597). The party included representatives of his Department and of DTI. The Japanese were investing more in health-related technology, like wrist-straps to monitor blood pressure and heart beat, so that a medical emergency could be anticipated and the patient moved to an A&E unit before it occurred. The importance of this was emphasised by the Royal Society of Edinburgh, who explained that where an elderly person found it difficult to go to the doctor or to a hospital, computer technology could be adapted for home medical care, so that for example a patient could use a digital thermometer or carry out blood pressure tests, and then communicate with a doctor who could interpret those measurements.[112]

5.60. The Royal Academy of Engineering also stressed the importance of early diagnosis in improving the effectiveness of the treatment of many life threatening conditions. Technology already exists which allows the monitoring of blood pressure, ECG, respiration etc using simple to operate devices and software by individuals carrying out basic monitoring of their own health in the home. The detection of changes in blood and tissue in the early stages could often lead to arresting or preventing further onset of disease, thus removing a significant burden from the NHS.[113]

5.61. There are obvious dangers in excessive reliance on remote monitoring. One less obvious risk is the potential for increased social isolation. When deciding whether to use these techniques in any individual case, this should be taken into account. Ease of use and avoidance of the need to travel are not the only considerations.

5.62. For the slightly more distant future, the Royal Academy of Engineering mentioned longer lasting artificial joints and new artificial organs (for example, portable kidney machines) as examples of new and specialised technologies which might come from the development in materials and ultra-precision engineering. Miniaturisation of electronics, wearable electronic monitors, and biocompatible electronics that can be implanted will help frail elderly people to be monitored remotely.

5.63. **The Department of Health's investment in assistive technology should be extended to include technologies and devices that can assist in monitoring health conditions and detecting early signs of health problems by individuals in the home.**

---

[112] p 390.

[113] p 122.

CHAPTER 6: INDUSTRY AND COMMERCE: THE MISSED OPPORTUNITY

6.1. The Prime Minister has said that "the demographic revolution offers challenges and opportunities for all of us", and that "for business, a changing customer base offers new markets".[114] In this chapter we examine the failure of business to confront this challenge and take advantage of these opportunities.

6.2. In Chapter 5 we noted the reluctance of car manufacturers to look at the buying power of older people who want to go on buying new cars; at how little attention is paid by industry to the needs of older people for electronic communication; and at the failure of industry to commit itself to the design and marketing of assistive technology. Each of these seems to us to be only one symptom of a generalised failure by industry and commerce to take advantage of the lucrative market represented by the ever-growing group of older people who have at their disposal what is sometimes called the Grey Pound.

6.3. Older people are often regarded as being the generation with the assets, and the leisure to spend those assets. This is an over-simplification. Mr Mervyn Kohler, the Head of Public Affairs at Help the Aged, made it plain that half of pensioners do not have a large enough income to pay tax, and that many are eligible for means-tested benefits (Q 457). Despite this, it is true that the UK's wealth, savings and spending power are now heavily concentrated within the over-50s. They hold 80% of all assets and 60% of savings, while over 75% of UK residents with assets of £50,000 or more are over 50. Some of the savings are tied up in the equities of their homes. Nevertheless, this group controls 40% of UK disposable income, making them a key group for buying in high-profile sectors such as cars, holidays and IT. They purchase 25% of all children's toys, and are the single biggest buyers of gifts at Christmas.[115]

6.4. The Committee heard oral evidence from Robert Diamond, the founder and chief executive of Diametric, a marketing agency. He told us that his company provided services to large national brand owners to help them in the effectiveness of their marketing, and three years ago had launched a unit to help mainstream brands understand and respond to the challenges of an ageing population. The unit had struggled to engage the large advertisers in the UK in a meaningful dialogue about the impact of an ageing population. One possible reason was that large advertisers and the marketers in the UK typically aimed at large families with children, and were genuinely concerned that marketing their products (whether cars, computers or food) overtly to an older audience might have the potential to alienate the mainstream; there was indeed some evidence that this was taking place. But perhaps more important was the fact that marketing was a youth sport: evidence from the Institute of Practitioners of Advertising suggested that 39% of UK marketing directors were aged under 35 and only 10% were over 50 (QQ 458-459).[116]

---

[114] Foreword to *Opportunity Age*, Cm 6466, March 2005.

[115] From the evidence of Mr Robert Diamond, p 268.

[116] From the evidence of Mr Robert Diamond, p 269.

6.5. Dr Nowell, from Age Concern England, did not think there was an awareness of the opportunities of engaging with the 50-plus population (Q 495). Professor O'Neill felt that companies had not woken up to the fact that there had been a change in the profile of their consumers, and gave us this example: "I remember running my first international conference on older drivers, and one of the automobile manufacturers gave me a grant towards it but said, "Don't mention we are supporting an older drivers' conference" (Q 378).

6.6. We do not single out industry for its apparently ageist attitudes, which sadly are common across all sectors of society. They are particularly evident in much of the output of major broadcasting organisations and of the print media. Although our inquiry has focused on scientific aspects of ageing, we have often been made aware of deeply entrenched negative attitudes to ageing and, by association, to older people themselves.

6.7. This prevailing attitude helps explain why, with a few notable exceptions, marketing directors start with the preconception that advertising and marketing should be targeted at the young. It does not explain why they should continue in this view when there is so much evidence of the potential market offered by older people. Mr Diamond added: "When we go round speaking to brand owners—and we work across almost all consumer sectors that you can imagine, from technology to automotive, to consumer goods to travel retail—everybody nods and looks at the numbers and is academically interested about the ageing population, but they then go back and do what they have been doing before." He thought the best solution might be more direct research and subsequent education among marketing practitioners, and he told us that the annual Older Richer Wiser conference of Haymarket Conferences, one of the largest organisers of conferences for the marketing community, was consistently sold out. It seemed to him that people were clearly looking for further information (QQ 463-466).

6.8. We are by no means the first to have noted this problem. In their December 2000 Report,[117] the Foresight Ageing Population Panel considered the opportunities and challenges for business and finance. They said:

"Businesses need to ditch outdated stereotypes about older consumers and focus on the grey pound, both in the UK and overseas. If they fail to grasp these new markets, overseas competitors will take advantage ... Businesses that plan on the assumption that tomorrow's older consumers and workers will simply be like today's will be wrongfooted by the effects of generational change ... As a matter of urgency, business organisations, trade associations and trades unions should raise the profile of ageing as a business issue and fill the information gap with industry-specific guidance. Assistance should be made available to firms to help them seize the new opportunities presented by an ageing customer base."

The Panel's recommendation was addressed to the Confederation of British Industry, Institute of Directors, Federation of Small Businesses, British Chambers of Commerce, trade associations, Trades Unions, and the DTI Small Business Service. Yet the evidence we have received shows that little has changed over the last five years.

---

[117] *The Age Shift – Priorities for Action*, pages 13-14.

6.9. We cannot understand why, with few exceptions, marketing directors of companies of every size seem unable to recognise the commercial opportunities which are there for the taking. Some of these are obvious, like remote controls for televisions and video recorders which can be used by those with poor manual dexterity or impaired vision. Manufacturers of mobile phones seem to concentrate on providing ever more complex functions for the young, rather than allowing older people to make use of their primary function.[118]

6.10. For older people, packaging raises special problems, not just of usability, but of safety. No less than 40,000 people are admitted to hospital every year for injuries sustained by trying to open packages using inappropriate instruments (Q 469).[119] Plastic packaging, especially of electrical goods, seems to be designed for the protection of the product and the manufacturer, without thought being given to the end user. A country which can build Concorde should surely be able to design jam jars and packets of peanuts which can be opened without a titanic struggle, or supposedly child-proof medicine packets which older people so often have to ask their grandchildren to open for them.

6.11. Perhaps there is a role here for the Design Council. We note that its website states that packaging can be viewed in four different ways: as a means of protecting the contents, as a contributor to the cost of the end product, as a sales canvas on which to promote the product's attributes and benefits, and as "a part of the product experience itself". An even more important function would be to enable the end user to derive maximum benefit from the product in return for minimum inconvenience.

6.12. Mr Kohler suggested that in a very competitive market the marginal cost of better packaging might deter manufacturers. A reason suggested by Mr Diamond was that manufacturers perhaps feared that appealing to older customers might alienate younger ones (Q 476). If these are the true reasons, it seems to us that not just manufacturing industry, but also the large suppliers who are in a position to dictate what they will buy and sell, are being remarkably short-sighted. We believe older people, and those shopping on their behalf, would readily pay a penny or two more for a product designed for easier use; and so might many younger shoppers.

6.13. Mr Diamond told us that in the United States there was a consumer body, the American Association of Retired Persons (AARP), which operated as a commercial and almost quasi-political body in influencing manufacturers to listen to and be responsive to the needs of an ageing population. Such a body was lacking in this country (Q 480). This is a matter which organisations representing consumers might consider. The University of the Third Age is building elements of what the AARP have achieved in the United States in terms of skills transfer and members (Q 486). We encourage them to continue to do so and in particular to be open to links with commercial organisations.

6.14. Our witnesses were unanimous in believing that the solution was not legislation or regulation, and we agree. We believe nevertheless that the DTI could use its influence to educate and train designers and marketers, and to

---

[118] See the evidence of Professor Newell quoted in paragraph 5.36.

[119] From the evidence of Mr Mervyn Kohler, Head of Public Affairs, Help the Aged, p 259.

bring to the attention of industry and commerce the opportunities open to them.

6.15. Dr Roger Orpwood, Deputy Director of the Bath Institute of Medical Engineering, suggested that if there were evidence of a burgeoning market, industry "would all be jumping on the bandwagon without any doubt whatsoever" (Q 238). We believe that the evidence is already there; the bandwagon is there; all that remains is for industry to jump on it. And if they do not, the view of the Royal Academy of Engineering is that "If we do not take action soon to co-ordinate our research, we could find ourselves missing out on a lucrative share in the fast growing market of the provision of the medical care solutions for the ageing population".[120]

6.16. We agree with Professor Tinker: "How come they do not see that older people want good design? ... Somebody is going to make a fortune when they do realise that there is this big market for good design." (Q 255)

6.17. **The Government's policy of encouraging older people to remain in their homes as long as possible will be thwarted if industry does not respond to this challenge.**

6.18. **The Government should consult with the Design Council, the Confederation of British Industry, the Institute of Directors, the Federation of Small Businesses, the British Chambers of Commerce, trade associations and trades unions on how they can best play an active part in developing these markets.**

6.19. **Like the Foresight Ageing Population Panel, we encourage manufacturers and the finance and services sectors to seize this opportunity simultaneously to benefit their older customers and their shareholders.**

---

[120] p 125.

CHAPTER 7: MANAGING HEALTH FOR OLD AGE

Introduction

7.1. Physical health is perhaps the most important factor to be considered in assessing the quality of life of older people, but it is only part of a wider picture. In this chapter we assess the role of the Department of Health, and the guidance it gives to the National Health Service. We next consider the involvement of other government departments, and how they coordinate their work. In this context, we look at the importance of a cross-departmental assessment of the cost-effectiveness of different approaches. Lastly we consider the role of older people in clinical trials, and the importance of longitudinal studies of ageing.

The National Service Framework for Older People

7.2. In March 2001 the Department of Health published the National Service Framework (NSF) for Older People. This is the main policy document of the Government, the Department and the NHS for dealing with the health of older people. The Department is to be applauded for recognising the need to make headway in what is still a relatively neglected area, and for attempting to move older people's services higher up the agenda.

7.3. We set out on page 72 the NSF for Older People, with the eight standards to be achieved.

7.4. At the time of the Wanless Report,[121] in addition to the NSFs for Older People and for Children, there were five disease-based NSFs governing coronary heart disease (CHD), cancer, renal disease, mental health services and diabetes. The review considered these disease-based NSFs in some detail,[122] and welcomed the Government's intention to extend the NSF approach to other diseases.[123] We accept that the disease-based NSFs have much to commend them. However, the NSF for Older People is not addressed only to clinicians; it is addressed to a much wider range of managers and clinicians in health, social care services and the independent sector, all of them crucial in developing an integrated service for older people. This is as it should be, but in broadening the aims, the hard edged evidence-based interventions and measurable health outcomes have been sacrificed to somewhat woollier objectives. The NSF is written in terms which are not sufficiently precise for it to be easy to verify whether or not a standard has been achieved.

---

[121] Final Report of the Review by Derek Wanless, *Securing our Future Health: Taking a Long-Term View*, April 2002.

[122] Paragraphs 2.32 to 2.61.

[123] Paragraph 2.33.

BOX 4

NSF for Older People: Standards

Standard One: NHS services will be provided, regardless of age, on the basis of clinical need alone. Social care services will not use age in their eligibility criteria or policies, to restrict access to available services.

Standard Two: NHS and social care services treat older people as individuals and enable them to make choices about their own care. This is achieved through the single assessment process, integrating commissioning arrangements and integrated provision of services, including community equipment and continence services.

Standard Three: Older people will have access to a new range of intermediate care services at home or in designated care settings, to promote their independence by providing enhanced services from the NHS and councils to prevent unnecessary hospital admission and effective rehabilitation services to enable early discharge from hospital and to prevent premature or unnecessary admission to long-term residential care.

Standard Four: Older people's care in hospital is delivered through appropriate specialist care and by hospital staff who have the right set of skills to meet their needs.

Standard Five: The NHS will take action to prevent strokes, working in partnership with other agencies where appropriate. People who are thought to have had a stroke have access to diagnostic services, are treated appropriately by a specialist stroke service, and subsequently, with their carers, participate in a multidisciplinary programme of secondary prevention and rehabilitation.

Standard Six: The NHS, working in partnership with councils, takes action to prevent falls and reduce resultant fractures or other injuries in their populations of older people. Older people who have fallen receive effective treatment and, with their carers, receive advice on prevention through a specialist falls service.

Standard Seven: Older people who have mental health problems have access to integrated mental health services, provided by the NHS and councils to ensure effective diagnosis, treatment and support, for them and for their carers.

Standard Eight: The health and well-being of older people is promoted through a coordinated programme of action led by the NHS, with support from councils.

7.5.   Most of the standards are however accompanied by "milestones" which were to be achieved by April 2005. By way of example, we set out in Box 5 the milestones for Standard Four of the NSF.

BOX 5

Milestones for Standard Four of the NSF for Older People

April 2002: All general hospitals which care for older people to have identified an old age specialist multidisciplinary team with agreed interfaces throughout the hospital for the care of older people. All general hospitals will have developed a nursing structure which clearly identifies nursing leaders with responsibility for older people. Consideration will have been given to Nurse Specialist/Nurse Consultant and Clinical Leaders (Modern Matrons).

April 2003: All general hospitals which care for older people to have completed a skills profile of their staff in relation to the care of older people and have in place education and training programmes to address any gaps identified.

The achievement of these milestones is unquantified. Progress is in practice assessed by asking a Trust or Primary Care Trust whether the standard is achieved, without specifying in detail what the criteria for success should be. It is all too easy for hospitals to claim that a standard has been met without any significant change having been made in clinical practice.

7.6.   In this respect the NSF for Older People may be contrasted with the NSF for CHD. There will for example be less room for argument as to whether a standard requiring "people with symptoms of a possible heart attack [to] receive help from an individual equipped with and appropriately trained in the use of a defibrillator within 8 minutes of calling for help" has or has not been achieved. In November 2004 DoH stated: "Since February 2000, nearly 700 [automatic external defibrilators] have been placed at 110 locations across England and more than 6,000 volunteers have been trained in Basic Life Support skills. Current evidence suggests that 57 lives have been saved as a direct result of the work of the programme." We would have hoped that the NSF for Older People might have included milestones in similar terms, for example in relation to thrombolyic therapy for acute stroke, target increases in hip replacements per thousand population of those aged over 75, or the percentage of acute stroke cases among older people admitted directly to a specialist stroke unit under a specialist consultant and team. There could be numerous other specific milestones.

7.7.   DoH witnesses were enthusiastic about the NSF for Older People. Mr Craig Muir, the Director of the Older People and Disability Division, listed a number of the specific milestones: "the introduction of integrated stroke services, the numbers of people treated for intermediate care, integrated falls services, protocols for dementia …rooting out age discrimination…" (Q 153). Although Mr Muir did not say so in so many words, the implication was that these had either been achieved, or were well on the way to being achieved. Certainly, in the case of stroke, Professor Fentem agreed that "Standard Five of the NSF for Older People has had its effect" (Q 290). We acknowledge that NSF standards have been helpful in raising awareness of the styles of desirable service, and in focusing the planning effort across the statutory and voluntary sectors. We are less convinced of their impact in improving health outcomes.

7.8. In support of the view that the NSF milestones were being met, Mr Muir cited a report to the Secretary of State from Professor Ian Philp, the National Director for Older People's Health, entitled *Better Health in Old Age* (Q 154). This was published by DoH only a few days before the departmental witnesses gave evidence to us on 9 November 2004. The report, which was accompanied by a "Resource Document", sets out the eight standards of the NSF which we have quoted in paragraph 7.2. It does not however consider whether or not they have been achieved, but describes "the progress that has been made since the NSF was published", and identifies "the major challenges and how these are being addressed". It sets out a series of case studies—there are more in the Resource Document—in which a number of persons describe the positive outcomes of their individual treatment at particular hospitals. These are good illustrative examples of the kinds of care that services should aspire to provide, but they do not supply hard evidence that the treatment of older people's conditions is improving.

7.9. The report does set out a number of matters where there have been significant improvements. Most of these are a consequence of the very welcome injection of funds into the NHS. Mr Muir told us that the report "does show a very strong improvement in a whole range of things. Also it shows areas where there is still a little way further to go, but the overall picture is one of dramatic increases, for example, the number of integrated stroke units increased from 45% to 90% … The number of people receiving intermediate treatment increased to 330,000 from just over 100,000, I think, over the period, so a quite substantial improvement". (Q 154) These are indeed welcome developments, and there are others listed in the report, such as increases in the numbers of consultants in old-age psychiatry and in old-age medicine. But it is impossible to tell to what extent these changes are simply a consequence of increased funding, and to what extent they follow from a clear and targeted application of scientific advances to the treatment of older people. We suspect that the answer is, more the former than the latter, particularly since no reference is made within the NSF for Older People to harnessing the developing insights from scientific research on age-related disorders.

7.10. The report concludes by stating as a fact: "Health in old age is improving and should continue to improve". This may well be true; we hope it is. But the evidence given for this is a table headed Summary of Progress (paragraph 3.1 of the report) showing increases in life expectancy at age 65, and decreases in the mortality rate from CHD, stroke, cancer and (in common with several other European countries) suicide. Since the table is contrasting figures for 1993 with those for 2002 and 2003, it is hard to see how they can be used to support the view that the NSF had, at the date of Professor Philp's report, played a significant part in this improvement.

7.11. Moreover, what is relevant is not an increased life expectancy, but an increased healthy life expectancy. It was Professor Sally Davies, the Department's own Director of Research and Development, who first drew our attention to the fact that HLE, far from keeping pace with LE, was lagging further and further behind (Q 139). We have seen no scientific evidence to support the proposition that health in old age is actually improving; what we have however seen is evidence that, whether or not their health is improving, older people perceive the last years of their lives as increasingly being years of poor health.[124]

7.12. Some of the disease-based NSFs deal with diseases prevalent in old age: CHD in particular, and to a lesser extent cancer and diabetes. Achievement of the milestones for those NSFs will therefore give an indication of the extent to which, in the case of those diseases, targets for older people have been achieved. We nevertheless believe that if there is to be a meaningful NSF dealing specifically with the health of older people, it must include targets making it possible to verify where progress has been made, and where further effort should be concentrated.

7.13. **The Department of Health must set out clear and measurable standards for assessing the health of older people, with particular emphasis on the care and treatment of those diseases prevalent in old age. Claims that those standards have been met should not be made unless they are supported by hard evidence.**

The importance of joined-up government

7.14. We have referred in this report to the involvement of many government departments in improving the quality of life of older people including (in addition to DoH) DTI and OST, DfT, ODPM, the Department for Education and Skills (DfES), and the Department for Culture, Media and Sport (DCMS).

7.15. If the quality of life of older people is to improve, there must be effective cooperation between all these departments. This was recognised in 1998, when the Prime Minister established an Inter-ministerial Group on Older People. In 2001 this was replaced by a Ministerial Sub-Committee on Older People (DA(OP)), a sub-committee of the Cabinet Domestic Affairs Committee.[125] The sub-committee's chairman is the Secretary of State for Work and Pensions. Until the general election the Secretary of State for Health was the only other departmental Cabinet minister member, but the Secretary of State for Trade and Industry has now been added. The sub-committee's terms of reference are "To develop and monitor the delivery of policy affecting older people; and report as necessary to the Ministerial Committee on Domestic Affairs."[126] We would have been interested to be told about the mechanism for ensuring implementation of the Committee's decisions.

7.16. Until the general election there was a second, and more senior, Cabinet Committee, MISC 29, which had as its terms of reference "To oversee and drive forward policy on the ageing society." In this committee the Secretaries of State for Health and for Work and Pensions were only two of nine Cabinet-rank ministers. We understand that this Committee was set up to deal with major projects concerning older people, and that at the date of this Report it is not proposed to appoint again a similar Cabinet Committee.

7.17. It was a Secretary of State for Social Services, Alistair Darling MP, who in April 2000 was appointed by the Prime Minister as the first "Government

---

124 Paragraphs 2.18 to 2.21

125 Since the general election, the name has been changed to "Sub-Committee on Ageing Policy".

126 Prior to the general election, the terms of reference were "To co-ordinate the Government's policies affecting older people; and to report as necessary to the Committee on Domestic Affairs."

Champion of Older People". That role was subsequently held by Alan Johnson MP, who until May this year was Secretary of State for Work and Pensions, and who, as we have said, chaired DA(OP). The choice for this task of the Secretary of State for Work and Pensions was re-affirmed in *Opportunity Age*, published by the Department for Work and Pensions (DWP) in March 2005.[127] Since the general election, the current Secretary of State for Work and Pensions, David Blunkett MP, has been appointed both as "Government Champion of Older People" and as chairman of DA(OP).

7.18. Given the choice of DWP as the coordinating department, and given that officials were in the course of preparing *Opportunity Age* while we were taking evidence for this report, we find it regrettable that they chose not to submit written evidence to us. In reply to our call for evidence, they explained that they felt they had nothing to contribute, and that other departments were better placed to offer evidence. It is true that many of the matters we are considering are the specific responsibilities of other departments, such as DoH, DfT, DTI and OST, all of which gave us written evidence, and oral evidence through their ministers and officials. But evidence from DWP on the coordination of departmental responsibilities would have been valuable.

7.19. *Opportunity Age* confirms that "at least seven different government departments have responsibility for major services directed to older people".[128] The paper is designed to bring together in one document all these responsibilities, including those of DfT and ODPM to which we referred in Chapter 5, those of DoH, and the responsibilities of the DTI and OST for research. We recognise that the economic aspects of old age, and pensions in particular, are at least as important as the medical and scientific aspects. If however the minister chosen to lead the Government's strategy for older people is to continue to be the Secretary of State for Work and Pensions, we believe that there are some matters which must remain the specific responsibility of other ministers and departments. We deal with these matters in Chapter 8.

7.20. **We welcome the appointment of a "Government champion of older people". We believe that this must be a single minister of Cabinet rank who, whatever his or her title and departmental responsibilities, has full responsibility for bringing together and implementing all aspects of government policy relating to older people.**

7.21. Although cooperation between departments leaves something to be desired, their cooperation with charities active in the ageing field seems to be good. Dr James Goodwin (for Help the Aged) and Dr Ian Nowell (for Age Concern England) both told us that they had positive experiences of working closely with DoH and DWP, and that they had found them to be very responsive. There was however more difficulty over their research plans and their strategic levels of spending (QQ 498-499).

Cost-effectiveness

7.22. For any individual suffering from some particular disease or condition, its rapid diagnosis, treatment and cure are plainly highly desirable. Even more desirable would be to avoid the disease or condition altogether. But although,

---

[127] Cm 6466, paragraph 5.5.

[128] Paragraph 5.3.

for the individual, prevention must always be better than cure, from a financial perspective this will not always be true. It is arguable that there comes a point at which too much money can be spent on the prevention of a condition which in any case has only a small chance of materialising. At that point, not only would the money not be well spent, but the portrayal of a risk factor as a disease might cause unnecessary fear of an unlikely consequence.[129] Despite this, we believe that an emphasis on prevention must normally be right.

7.23. At first sight, it seems plain that the resources of the NHS will also benefit if a lesser amount of money spent on prevention can save a larger of money which would have to be spent on treatment. In Chapter 4 we have given an example of this in relation to the positioning of scanners in stroke units. Other examples were given us. Professor Peter Weissberg took the view that "the major focus ... in terms of research has necessarily to be on the prevention of ... vascular disease in middle age, because ... if we could prevent the development of atherosclerosis in middle age then the consequences of vascular disease would be very much less in the elderly, and they would die of other things, in effect, because the organs involved are pretty robust." (Q 275)

7.24. We have however also been warned by Sir John Grimley Evans against adopting too simplistic an approach to the question of cost-effectiveness. There are two main reasons why, solely from the point of view of healthcare costs, prevention may not be cheaper than cure. The first is that the cumulative lifetime costs of prevention may exceed the cost of treatment in terms both of economics and fiscal accountancy. The second reason is the problem of competing morbidity: "One might avoid sudden death from a heart attack in one's fifties (cheap) only to survive a stroke in one's sixties (pretty expensive) or suffer Alzheimer's disease in one's seventies (very expensive)".[130]

7.25. In those cases where prevention and cure are both the responsibility of the NHS, it will be the NHS which is best placed to assess the long-term benefit of spending more money now on prevention to achieve a subsequent saving in the cost of treatment. But the NHS will not always be in the best position to judge. Money spent by the NHS now on prevention may result in savings—but not to the NHS—in long-term expenditure on care. Conversely, money saved to the NHS by avoiding treatment may result from expenditure on prevention elsewhere. Falls are a good example. We have already given[131] the startling figures for the frequency of falls among older people. Guidelines issued in November 2004 by the National Institute for Health and Clinical Excellence (NICE) are based on evidence showing that "falls are a major cause of disability and the leading cause of mortality resulting from injury in people aged over 75 in the UK. In 1999, there were 647,721 A&E attendances and 204,424 admissions to hospital for fall-related injuries in the UK population aged 60 years or over. The associated cost of these falls to the NHS and Personal Social Services was £908.9 million and 63% of these costs were incurred from falls in those aged 75 years and over".[132] However,

129 Iona Heath, British Medical Journal, 23 April 2005.

130 p 358.

131 Paragraph 4.27.

132 Scuffham and Chaplin, Incidence and Cost of Unintentional Falls of Older People in the United Kingdom.

savings in the costs to the NHS and personal social services would probably result mainly from expenditure outside the NHS, for example by local authorities.

7.26. Professor Weissberg explained it in this way:

"Again, we have all put forward economic arguments and mentioned "Is there a saving, ultimately, to be made?" The answer is yes, there is, but not to today's budget in that hospital. That is the way, I am afraid, the NHS looks at it; they are looking at this year's budget in this hospital: 'If I keep a heart failure patient out of that bed somebody else's patient is going to fill it.' So the bed is still filled, the work is still there, but in terms of future cost to the NHS there is a large saving, but we do not seem to have the flexibility to build that into the system." (Q 285)

7.27. That flexibility is vital. Government departments must look at the wider picture, and not assess it from the perspective of narrow departmental self-interest. It also seems to us plain that, where there is a possibility of saving even a fraction of these very large sums, an assessment of the cost-effectiveness of prevention must be a priority. Sadly, what we have discovered is that this question has not been addressed. In a document which looked at the most clinically and cost-effective interventions and rehabilitation programmes for the prevention of further falls, NICE stated that "a systematic review of the published literature up to August 2003 found no published cost effectiveness analyses of strategies for falls prevention in the elderly".[133]

7.28. **The initiation of studies of the cost-effectiveness of spending resources on prevention rather than treatment must be an important consideration for the Minister with overall responsibility for coordinating policy relating to older people.**

7.29. **There must be effective supervision to ensure that it is the overall cost to the taxpayer which is considered, and not the cost to the budget of an individual department, to the NHS or to local government.**

Clinical records

7.30. We were told by the Academy of Medical Sciences that the UK is strong in research into the fields of epidemiology, demography and population genetics, but that the potential for large-scale research of this kind has not been realised. The registration and record systems of the NHS could be an extremely useful resource for researchers, but the quality of data generated by the NHS is relatively poor. It has never matched the enormous research potential demonstrated by United States patient databases such as Medicare. Work in this area is inhibited by a confusing regulatory framework and a great deal of bureaucracy.[134]

7.31. **The Department of Health and the NHS should consult with the scientific community as to how the data generated by the NHS could be improved, the regulatory framework simplified, and the bureaucracy reduced.**

---

[133] Clinical practice guideline for the assessment and prevention of falls in older people, January 2005.
[134] p 192.

Clinical trials

7.32. Diseases associated with ageing are common targets for the development of new drugs and therapies, and older people often receive treatments for conditions which may strike regardless of age. Yet older people are commonly excluded from clinical trials; Professor Crome told us that this was why there were very few conditions for which we had a good evidence base of what treatments were required for the over-80s (Q 33). Reasons for such exclusion are not always explicitly stated, but when declared they may include the problems of co-morbidity, and the fact that an older person may already be taking other medications. Such exclusions make little sense scientifically. If a drug or therapy is to be used to treat an older person, who in all probability will have something else wrong with them and will be taking other medication, then the drug or therapy should be evaluated in these circumstances. Furthermore, from what is known already about the changes in physiology and metabolism that accompany ageing, the biological actions of a drug or therapy may be different in older people, and this needs to be assessed. The fact that older people may represent an intrinsically more variable target group is no justification for excluding them from clinical trials. The current position is like the man who searches for his lost keys under the streetlamp because "that way I can see what I'm doing", when in truth he knows he dropped them in the forest.

7.33. Two reasons are commonly given for the exclusion of older people from clinical trials.[135] The first is the alleged difficulty of obtaining their informed consent to participation. We do not believe that, except perhaps in the case of the oldest old, this in practice causes a problem. The second is that the bodies of older people metabolise drugs differently, which may distort research findings. It is precisely because this does "distort"—or, more accurately, influence—research findings that older people should be included in the trials. Only in this way will the effects of drugs on older people be reflected in the outcomes of trials. Since older people are increasingly the major users of drugs, it is most important that the pharmaceutical industry should as a matter of course include them in trials. The Medicines and Healthcare Products Regulatory Agency (MHRA) should ensure that this is done.

7.34. Professor Sally Davies explained that it was a concern of the Department of Health that trials should be open to people of all ages (Q 149). We commend this approach.

7.35. **The Department of Health and the research councils should take steps to ensure that older people are not routinely excluded from clinical trials, and that positive steps are taken to include them in the testing of medicines to be used to treat conditions prevalent among older people. The Medicines and Healthcare Products Regulatory Agency should ensure that the pharmaceutical industry does likewise.**

Longitudinal Studies of Ageing

7.36. We mentioned in Chapter 2 the importance of conducting longitudinal studies of ageing; this was also stressed by the Foresight Ageing Population

---

[135] Ferguson, *Selecting Participants when Testing New Drugs: the Implications of Age and Gender Discrimination*, Medico-Legal Society, April 2003.

Panel.[136] Longitudinal studies present obvious logistical challenges, and funding must be provided to support the necessary infrastructure over much longer periods of time than are required for cross-sectional surveys. Within the UK there have already been important longitudinal studies on scientific aspects of ageing such as the MRC Cognitive Functions and Ageing Study (CFAS) and the English Longitudinal Study of Ageing (ELSA). However, the range of questions that have been addressed remains limited, and each of these studies has experienced problems of continuity with its funding.

The Cognitive Functions and Ageing Study (CFAS)

7.37. CFAS is a large-scale epidemiological study of ageing with a special focus on cognitive and physical decline in later years. It is based on interviews with a random sample of persons aged 65 or over in six centres in England and Wales: Cambridgeshire, Gwynedd, Liverpool, Newcastle, Nottingham and Oxford. Three waves of interviewing were completed between 1990 and 2005.

7.38. The broad aims of the study are:

- to estimate the prevalence and incidence of cognitive decline and dementia and the variation throughout the country;

- to determine the natural history of dementia, in particular the rate of progression of cognitive decline;

- to identify factors associated with differing rates of cognitive decline and with the risk of dementia;

- to determine the contribution of different underlying pathologies to the rates of dementia, to the geographical variation in these rates and to the burden of disability; and

- to evaluate the degree of disability associated with cognitive decline, and the service needs this disability generates.

The English Longitudinal Study of Ageing (ELSA)

7.39. ELSA is based on a sample taken from the 1998 and 2001 survey years of the Health Survey for England. Eligible members of the sample were individuals born on or before 29 February 1952, and who therefore were aged 50 or over at the time of the start of the ELSA fieldwork. The 12,000 members of the sample completed questionnaires and were interviewed to provide data on such matters as health (including measurement of walking speed), housing, work, social participation, income, assets and pensions. A principal purpose of the survey is to examine the interrelationship between these different areas of life.

7.40. The data from all these interviews were published by the Institute for Fiscal Studies in December 2003 as the 2002 English Longitudinal Study of Ageing. A second wave of interviews of the same sample (as near as possible) took place in spring 2004, and subsequent interviews will take place every two years.

7.41. The value of such a survey is not confined to England. ELSA was designed to be compatible with the US Health and Retirement Study (HRS), and half

---

[136] *The Age Shift – Priorities for Action*, December 2000, page 25.

the funding for ELSA over the first five years has come from the US National Institute on Aging, the remainder being funded by nine Government Departments.[137] ELSA and HRS have become models for the Survey of Health and Retirement in Europe (SHARE) which is planned in several European countries to yield comparable data.

The funding problem

7.42. The strength of CFAS comes from its focus on detailed assessment of cognitive performance. It has included measures on other factors, including socioeconomic variables, but these have not been a major focus of enquiry. In the case of ELSA, its strength lies in the in-depth questioning on socio-economic matters such as work and retirement, social activity, physical and cognitive function, housing and social environment. However only one brief chapter deals with health problems, and therein lies its weakness. Whether the weaknesses of studies like CFAS or ELSA would best be addressed by extending their scope or by funding a network of interlinked longitudinal studies of ageing is a matter beyond the remit of this inquiry. Nevertheless, we have been made aware of the considerable importance of conducting longitudinal research on scientific aspects of ageing and of the major difficulties that investigators have encountered in securing the long-term infrastructure support that is needed to underpin such research.

7.43. **The Government should make additional funding available through the Department of Health and the research councils to implement joined-up programmes of longitudinal research on scientific aspects of ageing.**

---

[137] DfES, Defra, DoH, DTI, DWP, ODPM, Treasury, Inland Revenue, ONS.

CHAPTER 8: STRATEGIC DIRECTION AND CO-ORDINATION OF RESEARCH

Introduction

8.1. In this chapter we consider first the relationship between the learned societies, and the problem of the recruitment and retention of researchers. Next we look at public funding of research by government departments, by the European Union, by the research councils, and by the private sector. We then attempt to see what can be learned from the United States. Lastly and most importantly we consider what lessons can be drawn from this for the strategic direction and coordination of research in this country.

8.2. Different people and bodies have very differing views about what is covered by the umbrella word "ageing" in the context of research. The Wellcome Trust told us that they have no research programme for "ageing" as such, but "using a broad range of keywords to define ageing related research" they estimated that between 1994 and 2004 they spent 16% of their research budget funding £547m of research into ageing-related matters. However they had also made substantial investments in medical imaging technology and infrastructure support. If these were included, the total came to £877m, or 26% of their budget. This, they told us, was research directly or indirectly related to ageing, "using our broadest definition of ageing-related research".[138]

8.3. This illustrates the problem. If research can be broken down into the following categories:

(a) projects which have ageing as their primary focus;

(b) projects in which ageing is a secondary but nevertheless important factor; and

(c) projects which have only an incidental connection with ageing,

then in this chapter we are concerned with the first two of these categories, but not the third. These are only broad indications. We recognise that in the case of a number of projects there will be genuine differences as to which category they fall into, and this will be particularly true of the boundary between categories (b) and (c). Nevertheless we hope this illustrates what we have in mind. On this basis, we think it likely that most of the resources invested by the Wellcome Trust on research into medical imaging technology and infrastructure support would not have been spent on what we would call ageing research, though we have no means of knowing what proportion of the remainder would have fallen into category (a) and what into category (b).

8.4. Research into ageing is of course multidisciplinary, "ranging from the molecular and cellular changes associated with basic biological processes of cell death, senescence and physiological ageing, to technologies and design to help older people maintain their independence and autonomy."[139]

8.5. In the UK, public finance for this research comes mainly from four of the research councils, though some comes directly from government

---

[138] p 422.

[139] Research Councils UK, p 204.

departments. A substantial proportion comes from private foundations such as the Wellcome Trust and the Joseph Rowntree Foundation. Charities, many of them single-issue charities, are also large funders. The European Union has its own research programmes for ageing. Finally, a little funding comes from foreign countries (almost exclusively the United States); we have already mentioned the contribution made by the NIA to the funding of ELSA.[140]

8.6. In an ideal world, coordination would ensure the following:

- every worthwhile ageing-related research project would receive funding from at least one of these sources;

- no project would fail to receive funding solely because two funding organisations each thought that the project fell more closely within the responsibilities of the other;

- liaison within the UK between all the funding bodies, public and private, and with the European Union, would maximise the cost-effectiveness of funding by avoiding unnecessary duplication;

- liaison between UK and EU funders and funding bodies in other major countries would ensure that each was aware of the major projects being funded elsewhere in the world, and take account of this when deciding on the allocation of resources;

- major projects such as longitudinal studies would be compatible across different nations and cultures.

8.7. This of course is a counsel of perfection. But the picture we have received from the evidence falls so far short of the ideal that we believe radical measures must be taken to improve the current arrangements.

The learned societies

8.8. The first oral evidence we took was from representatives of three specialist learned societies. The British Geriatrics Society (BGS) is the UK learned society for doctors practising geriatric medicine. Most of its 2000 members are consultants and registrars practising geriatric medicine in the NHS. The 500 members of the British Society of Gerontology (BSG) are social scientists, sociologists and behavioural scientists. The British Society for Research on Ageing (BSRA) has 120 members, the majority of whom are academic scientists. It is concerned with the scientific study of biological ageing, and includes scientists from abroad who are interested in the causes and effects of the ageing process.

8.9. These societies therefore have different memberships and different aims, and the chairs of each of them told us that they regarded it as essential to continue to have three different societies representing the different disciplines. The societies nevertheless have a common interest in the ageing process, so that we were surprised to learn that they had not met together since 1996. We felt that, if three separate societies are to be retained, there should at least be close and frequent contact between them, and not just occasional informal contacts between some of the members (QQ 4-5). We were therefore delighted to learn that, following their meeting at the House

---

[140] Paragraph 7.41.

of Lords to give evidence to us, the chairs of these three societies met on 15 March 2005 and agreed to set up a forum of the three societies to act as a point of contact; to improve communication between them; to set up a small workshop to improve the impact of the learned societies upon policy making in the UK; and to collaborate to promote interdisciplinary training in gerontology, helping to meet the current gap in researchers able to work at the interface of social science, medical science and basic science in the field of ageing.[141] We commend this development.

Researchers

8.10. The "current gap in researchers" is a matter to which the three societies referred in their written and oral evidence. Professor Phillipson, the President of the BSG, told us: "... the problem with research capacity ... is a great concern, the fact that we do not have a clear ladder for researchers to go through and that people are lost, having been trained on particular projects. This is a waste of human capital which we really cannot afford to go on with ... I think that the Government does have a role in raising questions about where is the next generation of researchers going to come from ..."(Q 23). Professor Crome, President-elect of the BGS, thought that one reason was the paucity of suitably qualified academics. "We have gone in recent years from a situation where most medical schools had chairs or senior lecturers in geriatric medicine to a situation where there are an awful lot of vacant chairs. We do not have a large group of senior lecturers ready to take over the leadership roles, nor do we have a large number of people currently undertaking research training so they would be ready to take on roles in ten or 15 years' time ... For example, in the five London medical schools very soon there will only be two professors." (QQ 13-15)

8.11. A number of other witnesses expressed similar anxiety about the number of researchers beginning work on ageing, and about the associated lack of status accorded to them, and the poor financial rewards. Dr Goodwin, the head of research at Help the Aged, explained that very few researchers enter gerontology directly; most train in other disciplines and come to ageing after that. He felt that the absence of a sound career structure for scientists who wished to go into ageing research was a big impediment to maintaining quality and quantity. In geriatric medicine consultants had had their training reduced, and no longer had to do any research. We would be in very difficult circumstances in 15 to 20 years' time when the current tranche of researchers reached the ends of their careers (Q 489, Q 492, Q 508). For the Alzheimer's Society, Professor Clive Ballard was equally pessimistic: "... most promising PhD students are either moving to take up posts in industry or they are moving to the United States or other European countries, because there are more secure patterns of funding and there are better ways of helping people to develop their careers." (Q 317)

8.12. On our visit to the National Institute on Aging in Washington DC we were told by Dr John Hardy, Chief of the Laboratory of Neurogenics, who had himself moved from the UK to the United States in the 1990s, that he had recruited several researchers from research groups in the UK. Conditions for research in the United States were distinctly more attractive.[142] Plainly this

---

[141] Supplementary evidence submitted jointly by the BSRA, BGS and BSG, p 335.

[142] Appendix 5, paragraph 21.

constitutes another reason why young researchers may be reluctant to stay in the UK.

8.13. We are aware that this is not a problem unique to ageing research. Other subject areas also suffer from shortages of researchers. But we believe that in the case of ageing the problem is particularly acute. Research in this field does not yet have the same attraction as some other topics; it is more difficult to recruit researchers with qualifications in a number of disciplines; and the multidisciplinary nature of the research seems to make it more difficult to obtain funding.

8.14. It was suggested to us that the problems occasioned by the Research Assessment Exercise (RAE) might have contributed to the difficulty in attracting good quality researchers, in ageing and in other fields. The Academy of Medical Sciences said that it was "clear that the implementation of the Research Assessment Exercise has had some unfortunate side-effects, particularly the discouragement of the collaborative, inter-disciplinary and translational approaches upon which ageing research depends."[143] Another witness described the RAE as "particularly disastrous for scientific research into ageing".[144]

8.15. **Multidisciplinary and translational clinical research, which is particularly important for ageing, has been hampered by the Universities Research Assessment Exercise. The Higher Education Funding Councils should, as a matter of urgency, consider how this problem can best be addressed in the forthcoming Research Assessment Exercise.**

8.16. In written evidence, the BSG suggested that a solution to the shortage of researchers of the right quality might be post-doctoral fellowships promoted by the research councils and targeted at junior researchers. These offered an opportunity for expanding the number of researchers and promoting greater security in the profession. The BSG encouraged the expansion of this route as a relatively low-cost option for maintaining research capacity.[145]

8.17. Another possible way forward was suggested by Professor Robert Souhami, the director of policy and communication at Cancer Research UK. He explained that at the time Cancer Research UK was formed from the two previous charities, it had been decided to set up a training and career development board to make sure that there were no gaps in the training programmes of young laboratory and clinical scientists. That gave the charity strength in dealing with both the universities and the Royal Colleges, making sure that they regarded clinical career structures in the same way (Q 509).

8.18. Professor Souhami added that the focus on training and career development was an essential part of a funding agency's remit. We agree with this entirely. We believe that the diversity of disciplines represented in ageing research means that matters are not so straightforward as in the case of cancer research, which makes it all the more important that the issue of training should be a major responsibility of those in charge of coordinating funding. Who should be responsible for that coordination is the issue to which we now turn.

---

[143] p 194.

[144] Mr Frederic Stansfield, p 406.

[145] p 6.

Funding of research: government departments

8.19. The Department with the main responsibility for those aspects of ageing which concern us is the Department of Health. Its written evidence summarises the manner in which it supports research into ageing, and lists areas where research has been commissioned under the Policy Research Programme (PRP), the Health Technology Assessment Programme (HTA), and other research programmes. The PRP has promoted research into diseases specifically affecting older people, the influence of inequalities on morbidity and mortality, ways to prevent or reduce dependency, and research to increase understanding of the changing nature and needs of the ageing population. The HTA portfolio of work includes 67 studies related to the health and well-being of older people. In addition, research into ageing-related diseases is carried out under NHS Trusts, some of which have grouped together with local universities to form collaborative research groups. As at December 2002, DoH and the NHS together were committed to spending a total of £20.45m on 98 ageing-related research projects. Of this £4.8m was spent in 2002-03. However, according to Help the Aged this amounts to less than 1% of the NHS R&D budget.[146]

8.20. Not surprisingly for so broad a subject, a number of other government departments also finance research into ageing-related matters. We have already mentioned in Chapter 5 some of the research carried out by DfT, including the inquiry by the DVLA into age limits for driving licences. In 2002 DWP was committed to spending £3.57m on 18 projects, and in 2002-03 spent £1.23m.

Funding of research: the research councils

8.21. By far the greater part of funding for ageing-related research comes not directly from government departments but from the research councils. They are the responsibility of the Office of Science and Technology (OST), part of DTI. Research Councils UK (RCUK), the "strategic partnership which champions the research supported by the seven UK Research Councils"[147] explained that the following four research councils are involved:

> Biotechnology and Biological Sciences Research Council (BBSRC);
>
> Engineering and Physical Sciences Research Council (EPSRC);
>
> Economic and Social Research Council (ESRC);
>
> Medical Research Council (MRC).

They "are key public sector funders in basic and applied research relevant to ageing (as a natural process), covering a broad remit, ranging from the molecular biology of ageing processes to the built and local environment, transport and the social and economic aspects of growing old. The Research Councils not only fund research specific to ageing, but also a considerable amount of relevant research into individual diseases, physiological systems, and technology."[148]

---

[146] p 283.

[147] p 196.

[148] p 196.

8.22. In their original evidence, RCUK summarised the spend by the research councils on ageing-related research programmes live on 31 July 2002. The figures for 2002 were subsequently updated with equivalent figures for 31 July 2004.[149] The annualised spend on each programme was calculated as the total cost divided by the duration. If a project was relevant to ageing it was included as 100% of its costs "even if the research was diverse, and ageing was only one aspect of it".[150] Inevitably this definition gives a generous estimate of the amount spent on ageing research.

8.23. In the table below we give the amount spent by each of the four research councils on ageing-related research in 2002 and 2004; the budget allocation of each of them for 2004-05; and the percentage of that allocation spent on ageing-related research:

TABLE 6

Research Council Spend on Ageing Research

Figures in £m	BBSRC	EPSRC	ESRC	MRC	Total RC
July 2002 spend	8.9	3.3	1.3	115.0[151]	128.6
July 2004 spend	15.3	6.5	1.3	128.0	151.1
Allocation 2004-05	287.6	497.3	105.2	455.3	1,345.4
% on ageing research	5.3 %	1.3 %	1.2 %	28.1 %	11.23 %

8.24. Each research programme is assigned to one of ten following categories:

(1)   The economics, psychology and sociology of ageing and the life-course;

(2)   The economic, social and policy implications of an ageing population;

(3)   Technologies and design to help people maintain their independence and autonomy; (and the effects of those technologies);

(4)   Technologies for the detection, prediction diagnosis and treatment of age related diseases (and the effects of those technologies);

(5)   The molecular and cellular changes associated with basic biological processes of cell death, senescence and physiological ageing;

(6)   The causes of, and influences on age related diseases and disability;

(7)   Prevention of breakdown in health and loss of independence in old age and of specific diseases and conditions which cause these;

(8)   Treatments for disease and the breakdown in health in older people;

(9)   Rehabilitation strategies to improve and maintain function and restore independence;

---

[149] p 217.

[150] p 205.

[151] The figures for the MRC spend in 2002—and hence also for the total spend—have with the agreement of RCUK been adjusted from those originally given in evidence (see p 203) to include spend on Units/Institutes and on stand-alone fellowships. This makes the figures directly comparable with those for 2004.

(10)   The delivery of effective and efficient health and social care for old and frail people.

8.25. Over half the spend of the MRC is in category 6, with most of the rest divided between categories 5 and 8. Most of the BBSRC spend is in category 5; the EPSRC spend is divided between categories 4 and 8, and the ESRC spend goes mainly on work in category 1, with a lesser proportion to category 2.

8.26. RCUK provided us with extensive written evidence, and also with supplementary written evidence, for which we are most grateful.[152] We also had the benefit of oral evidence on behalf of each of these four research councils.[153] Our impression from this evidence is of considerable diversity in their approaches to the topic. The EPSRC have the EQUAL initiative (Extending the Quality of Life) which was praised by Professor Peter Lansley at our Seminar for its work in creating better home and hospital environments, and in supporting assistive technology.[154] Likewise the two initiatives of the BBSRC—SAGE (Science of Ageing) and ERA (Experimental Research on Ageing)—have helped to stimulate growth and to draw researchers from other branches of science to develop interests in ageing.

8.27. It is more difficult to evaluate the work of the MRC. On the face of it, the MRC appears to devote large sums to ageing-related research. We believe that these figures considerably over-estimate the importance which the MRC actually attaches to ageing research. The fact that a project is classed as relevant to ageing, and that 100% of its costs are included "even if the research was diverse, and ageing was only one aspect of it", seems to us to produce figures which are considerably inflated. We are supported in this view by looking at the lengthy list of projects sent to us in February 2005 by RCUK.[155] Although no conclusion can be drawn from the title of an individual project, the titles of the full list of 338 projects leave us with the distinct impression that many have only a minor or even marginal connection with ageing.

8.28. We have no similar problems in evaluating the work of the ESRC. At a time when the psychology and sociology of ageing, and their associated policy implications, are of increasing importance, we find it astonishing that the ESRC should spend scarcely 1% of its allocation, amounting to £1.3m, on scientific research on these important topics. This point was specifically put to Professor Ian Diamond, the chief executive of the ESRC, when he gave oral evidence (QQ 443-444). We were not persuaded by his reply, and can see no possible justification for this very low level of spending.

8.29. **We recommend that the Economic and Social Research Council should urgently and significantly increase the proportion of its funding available for ageing-related research. The Director-General of Research Councils should supervise this.**

---

[152] p 196 , p 234.

[153] p 219.

[154] See Appendix 4, paragraphs 28-32.

[155] This is not printed in the evidence volume.

8.30. The research councils make grants for the funding of research projects on the basis of assessments by grant-awarding panels. The effectiveness of the peer review process depends on these panels being composed of scientific experts knowledgeable in the relevant field. In the case of both the MRC and the BBSRC, only a handful of the members of the councils and their scientific committees have expertise at all closely connected with ageing. This lack of expertise extends to the Strategy Boards and training awards committees as well as to the response-mode funding mechanisms. This is in sharp contrast to the position in the United States, where funding applications to the National Institute on Aging are invariably reviewed by experts selected for their knowledge of the scientific aspects of ageing.

8.31. Professor Linda Partridge conceded that this lack of expertise caused problems with groups trying to obtain follow-on funding through the responsive mode committees in the BBSRC. In the case of ageing there had been a very low success rate. It was possible that the multidisciplinary nature of the ageing proposals did not appeal to committees that had specific expertise in biochemistry, structural biology or genetics because ageing was not confined to any one of those topics. She thought that this was something the Council needed to address (Q 403). We agree.

8.32. **The research councils should ensure that when their scientific committees are considering applications for funding for ageing-related research, they include a majority of members with specific experience in these fields.**

Funding of research: the European Union

8.33. Some funding of research, and coordination within the member states, is done through the EU. The Fourth Framework Programme for Research (FP4) ran from 1994 to 1998. Of the total of €13.25 billion spent on research, €157m went on biomedicine and health, though it is hard to estimate how much of this might be classed as ageing-related research. In the Fifth Framework Programme (FP5), from 1998 to 2002, out of €14.96 billion spent on research, €190m was spent on Key Action 1 (Quality of Life) and Key Action 6 (Ageing and Disability). The current Framework Programme, FP6, runs from 2002 to 2006, and does not have a specific heading for ageing and disability research. Out of a total of €17.5 billion, €1,155m is being spent on combating major diseases, but again it is not clear what proportion of this is spent on ageing research.

8.34. On 6 April 2005 the EU Commission announced the proposal for a Seventh Framework Programme (FP7) to run for seven years from 2007 to 2013. Under the first main theme, Health appears this sub-heading:

Research on the brain and related diseases, human development and ageing: to explore the process of healthy ageing and the way genes and environment interact with brain activity, under normal conditions as well as in brain diseases.

There is as yet no means of knowing how much of the €8.3 billion proposed for Health research may be spent on this sub-head, but there have already been calls[156] for research on ageing to be made a priority.

---

[156] For example from Mr Lambert van Nistelrooij MEP, co-President of the European Parliament's Intergroup on Ageing.

8.35. In the context of FP7, the Commission has proposed the setting up of a European Research Council, with the power to awards grants totalling €2 billion annually. At this stage a five-person committee, chaired by Lord Patten of Barnes, is in the process of identifying possible members of the governing body of the Research Council who would guarantee its autonomy and its focus on excellence in research.

8.36. **The Government must ensure that a very significant proportion of the resources allocated to the EU Seventh Framework Programme is set aside for ageing-related research. Members of the European Parliament should also press for this.**

Funding of research: the private sector

8.37. The Wellcome Trust is by far the largest medical charity in the UK. As we said at the start of this chapter, it does not break down its research spend into ageing-related research, but the figures cited there show that something of the order of £50m of its annual research budget is spent on this. From figures available in December 2002, the Joseph Rowntree Foundation was then funding projects worth £1.25m, and the Nuffield Foundation £0.29m.

8.38. Help the Aged is the only charity concerned solely with older people which sponsors an appreciable volume of scientific research. Through its research arm Research into Ageing, in 2002 it was spending £2.45m per annum sponsoring projects worth a total of £5.04m. Expenditure on projects current in 2002 sponsored by single-issue charities concerned with diseases prevalent in old age was:

Stroke Association	£5.98m
Alzheimer's Society	£ 2.3m
British Heart Foundation	£ 1.4m.

Cancer Research UK has a very much larger research budget, but this of course covers a variety of cancers spread over all ages, so that the figures are not directly comparable.[157]

8.39. During the visit to Washington DC which we describe below we had the opportunity to visit the Ellison Medical Foundation, one of the major private funders in the United States of research into ageing.[158] The distinguishing feature of the Foundation is that it is funded by a philanthropist who takes a great personal interest in what it does. The Foundation is therefore accountable only to him, and can afford to fund projects which bear a high level of risk or are likely to bring results only in the long term. Funding can be awarded on the basis of applications only a few pages long, and this leads to exceptionally low administrative costs. We were most impressed by the Foundation's work, but we doubt whether parallels can be drawn with funding by charities in this country.

Coordination and collaboration: the current position in the UK

8.40. It hardly needs to be said that there must be coordination between all these manifold publicly-funded sources of research funding. And although the

---

[157] Help the Aged, p 298.

[158] A full report of the visit is at Appendix 5, paragraphs 3-18. See also paragraph 3.53 above.

taxpayer (as opposed to individual taxpayers) plays no part in the funding spent by private foundations and by charities,[159] it is also in everyone's interest that there should be collaboration between those responsible for publicly and privately funded research. We therefore looked to see what arrangements for such coordination were in place. We found that there were or had recently been in place a number of bodies responsible for various aspects of coordination.

8.41. The **Cross-Council Coordinating Committee on Ageing Research (XCAR)** was established in May 2000, the key aims being to encourage the development of research activities across the research council boundaries, and to ensure that consideration of multidisciplinary research proposals are coordinated across the councils. If one of its purposes is to give prominence to ageing among multidisciplinary programmes supported by the research councils, we fear that it has not been successful. RCUK sent us a copy of a lengthy memorandum on Interdisciplinary Research which it submitted on behalf of the research councils to the Council on Science and Technology in 2004. Annex 1 contains a seven-page summary of cross-Research Council multidisciplinary activities with not a single reference to ageing, even in the section on genomics.

8.42. XCAR has been instrumental in establishing both the National Collaboration on Ageing Research and the New Dynamics of Ageing cross-Council research programme. We now consider these.

8.43. The **National Collaboration on Ageing Research (NCAR)** was an initiative launched with a major conference in November 2001 and funded via XCAR. It was initially funded for three years, up to 31 January 2005. The key aim of NCAR was to stimulate interdisciplinary research in the field of ageing through workshops in key areas, networking and dissemination. The effectiveness of NCAR was evaluated by an independent panel (the Cross Research Council Evaluation Panel for the National Collaboration on Ageing Research), which reported in critical terms in the autumn of 2004. The panel concluded that there was no longer a need for NCAR, and this recommendation was accepted by the research councils at a meeting on 25 October 2004. The funding of NCAR was accordingly not continued beyond 28 February 2005.

8.44. It did not come as a surprise to us to hear this, since the evidence we received on NCAR was less than enthusiastic. The Biosciences Federation told us that "national coordination to date has been largely ineffective at the research level, despite the creation of NCAR".[160] In the opinion of the BSRA executive, NCAR was "largely unsuccessful".[161] The Centre for Ageing and Public Health of the London School for Hygiene and Tropical Medicine said: "The Collaboration seems to have had too little resource to make a significant difference."[162] The view of Dr S Brownsell and Professor M.S.Hawley (Barnsley General Hospital) was that NCAR and the Funders'

---

[159] If one excepts that, in the case of charities, 22/78ths or 28% of money donated by Gift Aid has since 2000 accrued to the charity rather than to the Revenue.

[160] p 330.

[161] p 9.

[162] p 347.

Forum to date "appear to have had little impact on coordination in the field of assistive technology".[163]

8.45. Oral evidence was to the same effect. Dr Diana Dunstan, Director of the Medical Research Group of the MRC and chair of XCAR said: "They [the National Collaboration for Ageing Research] have not achieved as much, as we have all said, in directing or encouraging the community to send to the research councils really good multi-disciplinary applications, which was what we were looking for. The way they had approached it had not been as successful as we hoped." (Q 428) Lord Sainsbury of Turville, the Minister for Science, when asked whether NCAR had not been found to be ineffective, replied: "I think the general feeling was that it had not been totally ineffective ... it is not correct to say that it had totally failed. It had done some good work". (QQ 528-9) This was hardly a ringing endorsement.

8.46. One of the reasons the panel which evaluated NCAR was not unhappy about recommending that its funding should be discontinued was that it believed another body was well placed to take on NCAR's activities. This body was the **Funders' Forum for Research on Ageing and Older People (FFRAOP**, or, when there is no possibility of confusion with other Funders' Fora, simply the **Funders' Forum**) which was also set up in 2001. Its aim was to extend the existing collaboration between the four research councils (BBSRC, EPSRC, ESRC and MRC), bringing them together with six major charities and the Department of Health. In theory it meets once a year to receive reports from its members and to make recommendations for research and development. In practice it has not met since June 2003.[164] It has advisory powers only. In a research strategy document issued in October 2003, Dr James Goodwin, the head of research of Help the Aged, said that the Funders' Forum "has been perceived as lacking leadership, coherence and unified and purposeful effort." In written evidence to us, Help the Aged said that the Forum "lacks the authority to direct a national agenda".[165]

8.47. If the Funders' Forum is also to assume some of the responsibilities of NCAR, plainly it must have the confidence of the research community. The evidence does not show this. Professor Peter Fentem, speaking for the Stroke Association, told us that he had been a member of the Funders' Forum, but that it had been "particularly disappointing" (Q 287). The Centre for Ageing and Public Health of the London School of Hygiene and Tropical Medicine believes that "the Forum has had a modest effect at best".[166] The view of RCUK is: "The Funders' Forum is a large and somewhat unwieldy body due to the nature of the field it covers. Despite their common focus on ageing, the principal funders constitute a very wide spectrum with different missions, which has inevitably created challenges. To date, it has mainly been a forum for discussion and exchange of views. The diversity of the FFRAOP distinguishes it from other Funders' Fora, such as those in the cancer and cardiovascular fields, which are able to make more of an impact because they are smaller and more tightly focussed."[167]

---

[163] p 341.

[164] Supplementary written evidence from Dr Stephen Ladyman MP, a former Parliamentary Under Secretary of State at the Department of Health, p 325.

[165] p 284.

[166] p 347.

[167] p 201.

8.48. RCUK also told us that the Funders' Forum "is currently reviewing its role". They subsequently explained that a sub-group, the Business Planning Group, had met six times between October 2002 and January 2004, and agreed on the need for a dedicated programme manager to take the work forward. Ideally this would be a full-time post, initially for three years. Despite pledges from the research councils and the health departments for contributions towards the cost, by April 2005 there was still insufficient money to support the post. RCUK hoped that this would be resolved when the Funders' Forum reconvened.

8.49. The view of RCUK as to the successful coordination of cancer research was borne out by Professor Souhami of Cancer Research UK: "There is within the UK a very successful forum where the funding partners get together. That is the National Cancer Research Institute. In the National Cancer Research Institute, the major funders of cancer are sitting and discussing the questions of research priorities in cancer. Cancer Research UK is there, the Department of Health is there, the Medical Research Council, the Leukaemia Research Fund, Wellcome and so on. There is now a national forum for considering issues which relate to research priorities as they affect cancer." (Q 489) This shows that, given the right organisation, successful coordination is perfectly feasible.

8.50. The **New Dynamics of Ageing Programme (NDA)** is not a coordinating body, but aspires to be a cross-council programme to coordinate ageing research. It was announced in 2004 as a £12m initiative of the ESRC, with the support of the EPSRC, BBSRC and MRC. The former director of NCAR was appointed as director of the NDA. We asked RCUK how the NDA would overcome the factors that led to NCAR falling below expectations. They pointed out that NCAR was a networking activity and not a research programme like the NDA. The research councils were "planning a number of steps to ensure that the performance of NDA [would] fully meet expectations in every area of its remit". It would have management mechanisms for assessing progress, none of which were in place for NCAR. Thus, to support the director there would be an advisory committee made up of academics from across the range of disciplines. Key performance indicators would be developed against which the programme could be monitored through annual reports and twice-yearly meetings with the programme case officer and a nominated liaison member from the ESRC Strategic Research Board.[168]

8.51. RCUK told us that a central objective of the NDA would be "to encourage and support the development of innovative interdisciplinary research groups and methods with the aim of helping to create a new generation of interdisciplinary researchers", and "to provide a sound evidence base for policy and practice (including the development of prototype systems, procedures and devices) so that research contributes to well-being and quality of life".[169]

8.52. In evidence to us on 8 February 2005 Professor Ian Diamond told us: "… we are all extremely excited about the New Dynamics of Ageing Programme that we are just about to start commissioning …" (Q 388). Age Concern England welcomed the NDA, believing that it would give "a real

---

[168] p 245.

[169] p 203.

collaboration between the research councils"(Q 489). But this view, and the excitement of Professor Diamond, are not yet shared by the research community. At that date, 9 months after it had been announced, the NDA had yet to issue a call for research proposals. The first such call was published on the ESRC website on 12 April, but this was for short expressions of interest only. Programme grants are to be commissioned only from early 2006. This will be 18 months after the launch of the NDA was announced.

8.53. We asked the research councils to explain the reasons for the delay. Their response was:

"The commissioning of a research programme runs through several stages the first of which is the publication of the call. Whilst the intention to commission the New Dynamics of Ageing Programme (NDA) has been public on the ESRC website this has been for the prime purpose of generating interest within the scientific and user community in advance of the programme actually being commissioned. Since then we have been working to ensure the most effective commissioning of this multi-disciplinary programme. In order to ensure a transparent, fair and robust process, with opportunities for cross-council working, the commissioning of a programme of this scale is carefully worked out and staged. It is for this reason that phase I funding decisions will be taken early next year."

We do not understand why transparency, fairness and robustness require such a very long delay before the first funding decisions can be taken.

8.54. The consequence however is that, for the present, only two of these four bodies are in any way active. Of these two, XCAR coordinates only the work of the research councils. Only the Funders' Forum has a remit to coordinate ageing-related research more widely but, as we have said, it last met in June 2003, and it does not appear to command the confidence of the research community.

8.55. We are not alone in believing that coordination of ageing research in this country is singularly lacking. Even from within the research councils, there was criticism. Professor Linda Partridge, the Weldon Professor of Biometry at University College London, speaking on behalf of the BBSRC, gave us these examples. "There are various small rules which turn out to be major obstacles if one is trying to put together an interdisciplinary team, which is often what is needed for a research programme in ageing. For instance, the BBSRC are not allowed to fund work on disease... There can also be collaboration issues, so people, for instance, in MRC units cannot easily obtain joint funding with people trying to get money through the EPSRC or the BBSRC through a responsive mode. There are a number of such barriers which are a problem specifically for ageing research, I think, because of the need for interdisciplinarity." (Q 418)

8.56. No evidence that we have received, written or oral, has been enthusiastic about the current arrangements for coordination. By contrast, some of the views we have received are less than enthusiastic:

- Academy of Medical Sciences: "Research into ageing is poorly coordinated in the UK."[170]

---

[170] p 194.

- Royal Academy of Engineering: "…the UK has not generally been good at cross-Research Council funding."[171]

- Biosciences Federation: "National coordination to date has been largely ineffective at the research level, despite the creation of [NCAR]. There are two types of deficiencies: translating research discoveries made under the remit of one Research Council to clinical research sponsored by a second Research Council; and securing funding for work that currently falls between the remits of two Councils."[172]

- Pocklington Trust: "From our perspective, there appears to be a lack of leadership at national level on dissemination of research into policy and practice."[173]

8.57. Views on coordination between the public and private sectors were mixed:

- Professor Cyrus Cooper: "The research councils do not, to our knowledge, have a particularly coordinated approach to musculoskeletal disease between, say, the BBSRC, MRC let alone bringing in the Wellcome Trust and the charities." (Q 54)

- Royal Academy of Engineering: "Private and public research has been reasonably co-ordinated and the charitable sector has been closely involved in the human factors aspects."[174]

- Biosciences Federation: "BBSRC and EPSRC have had some success in integrating their research programmes with those of the major charities funding ageing research. The BBSRC's Experimental Research on Ageing programme, for instance, includes observers from the charity Research into Ageing." [175]

- Royal College of Physicians of Edinburgh: "We also suggest that there should be an attempt to facilitate greater of co-ordination of research than hitherto between the public, private and charitable sectors."[176]

8.58. **Our conclusion is that the attempts at coordination so far made under the aegis of the research councils are woefully inadequate. The image we have is of a series of ill-thought-out initiatives which have long titles, short lives, vague terms of reference, little infrastructure, and no sense of purpose. A radical reorganisation is essential.**

8.59. This reorganisation of research coordination is the problem to which we now turn.

Coordination of research in the United States

8.60. A number of the witnesses who, like us, came to the conclusion that a radical change was needed to provide proper coordination of research in this country drew comparisons with the organisation of research into ageing in the United States. They suggested the setting up in this country of an organisation

---

[171] p 125.

[172] p 330.

[173] p 409.

[174] p 125.

[175] p 330.

[176] p 392.

modelled on the National Institute on Aging (NIA). We therefore visited the NIA on 18 and 19 January 2005. A full report of our visit is attached as Appendix 5.

8.61. The National Institute on Aging is one of the 27 institutes making up the National Institutes of Health (NIH), based in Bethesda, a suburb of Washington DC. Congress granted the authority for the setting up of the institute in 1974. The purpose is to provide leadership in ageing research, training, health information dissemination, and other programmes relevant to ageing and older people. Subsequent amendments designated the NIA as the primary federal agency for Alzheimer's disease research.

8.62. For the financial year 2005 the NIA has an appropriation of $1.05 billion, an increase of 3% over the previous financial year. One tenth of this is spent on the NIA's own intramural programme, conducting basic and clinical research on the NIH campus in Bethesda, and in Baltimore, but the NIA's primary task is to finance extramural research in the United States and, to a very limited extent, elsewhere.[177] There are four extramural programmes funding research and training at universities, hospitals, medical centres, and other public and private organisations nationwide. They are the Biology of Aging Program, the Behavioral and Social Research Program, the Neuroscience and Neuropsychology Program, and the Geriatrics and Clinical Gerontology Program.

8.63. The NIA is accountable to Congress for the use of the funds voted for it. Its mission is very broad, and the appropriation comes with little specificity as to the use to be made of it. For the quality of its research, the NIA is accountable to a National Advisory Council on Aging, which advises the Secretary of the Department for Health and Human Services, the Assistant Secretary for Health, and the Directors of the NIH and the NIA. The Council meets three times a year to consider applications for research and training, and to recommend funding for those applications that show promise of making valuable contributions. The Council also makes recommendations to the Director of the NIA regarding research conducted at the Institute.

8.64. The Centre for Ageing and Public Health made the following comparison of funding methods in the UK and the United States:

---

[177] We refer in paragraph 7.41 to the fact that ELSA is in part funded by the NIA.

BOX 6

Funding of Research in the United Kingdom and the United States

The UK arrangements for funding research relevant to an ageing population remain fragmented and arguably unfocused. This may be contrasted with the US National Institute of Aging: The point is not so much the size of its annual budget of one billon dollars. Rather, the NIA conducts and supports an extensive program of research on all aspects of aging, from the basic cellular and molecular changes, through the prevention and treatment of common age-related conditions, to the behavioural and social aspects of growing older, including the demographic and economic implications of an aging society. Thus the NIA covers the research agenda that is the responsibility in the UK of all the Research Councils and the Department of Health (excepting the design and technology research of the EPSRC). In consequence, the US has a far more coherent effort in the field than does the UK.[178]

8.65. Three points seem to us to be especially relevant to any consideration of modelling coordination of research on this country on the NIA. The first is that the NIA is only one of 27 institutes within the NIH. All other research in any way connected to health matters is organised in the same way. The NIH is in a position to oversee any differences between these institutes, any difficulties over the allocation of funds, and any overlap of or gaps in funding. We doubt whether it would be possible to set up a body with the same features as the NIA without making comparable changes to the organisation of research in many other fields. This may be thought to be desirable, but it is not a matter within our remit; we have received no evidence on it, and it would plainly have far-reaching consequences which we have not considered. In the absence of a body with the overarching responsibilities of the NIH, the setting up of an institute governing only one aspect of health research seems to us to be fraught with difficulty.

8.66. Another major problem would be the funding of research. As we have said, the main responsibility of the NIA is the funding of extramural research, which in this country is primarily the responsibility of the research councils. A recommendation for the setting up of an NIA-type body would be tantamount to recommending the establishment of an additional Ageing Sciences Research Council which, using funds at present administered by four of the research councils (and primarily the MRC), would be exclusively responsible for grants for ageing-related research (however defined), to the exclusion of the other research councils. This might have advantages, but we doubt whether it could be done without a wholesale reorganisation of all the work of the research councils. At present they are based on scientific disciplines. This has its own logic, but inevitably causes difficulties for all research topics (not just ageing) which straddle more than one discipline. If all research councils allocated funds on the basis of subjects rather than discipline, this too would be logical, though it would have inevitable concomitant difficulties in the case of research in one discipline covering more than one subject. What would, it seems to us, cause the most difficulty would be to have, in addition to the present discipline-based research

---

[178] p 347.

councils, one council responsible for all the research in one multidisciplinary subject.

8.67. The last consideration is the question of intramural research. We were told on our visit to the NIA that one of its strengths is that, because it undertakes itself a considerable volume of research, those allocating funds for extramural research have a better idea of what projects are likely to be worth funding. This does indeed appear to be a considerable asset, but the essential feature is surely that those responsible for funding should have current or recent first-hand experience of undertaking research, wherever that research is undertaken. That should be the position of the research councils in this country.[179] The fact that they undertake only a little intramural research on ageing does not seem to us to cause any insuperable difficulties.

8.68. We are moreover conscious that any recommendation for the setting up at this stage of a new intramural research facility would involve very great expenditure, and that the recruitment of the necessary researchers would inevitably impact unfavourably on existing research facilities. The choice of projects to be undertaken at the new facility would also affect extramural projects on similar topics and might well be seen, rightly or wrongly, to favour the intramural facility.

8.69. The NIA has a universally acknowledged exceptional and enviable reputation for the organisation and coordination of ageing research in the United States. For the reasons given in the previous paragraphs it does not seem to us to be essential or even practicable to set up a similar body in this country. The challenge is to find a method of coordinating research in this country which, without fully reflecting the position in the United States, can nevertheless achieve the same ends, and in time earn the same reputation.

Coordination and collaboration: the future for the United Kingdom

8.70. In this country the research councils alone spend £150m a year of taxpayers' money on ageing research, broadly defined. Ultimate responsibility for the effective use of these resources, and hence for the coordination of this research, must lie with a government department and with a senior Minister responsible to Parliament for the use of these funds. That department can take a strategic view of the whole topic.

8.71. Which government department should be responsible? There seem to us to be three possibilities. The first is DWP. As we explained in the previous chapter,[180] it is the Secretary of State for Work and Pensions who has been chosen by the Government as the Government's Champion for Older People. Whatever the qualifications for that title of the holder of that office, it seems to us that DWP has no serious role to play in the coordination of scientific research, and we mention that department here only for completeness.

8.72. A second possibility is the Department of Health, which is of course responsible for the NHS, for the health of the population, and specifically for the health of older people. It also has its own research programmes which need to be coordinated with the rest. Many, probably most, of the relevant

---

[179] See our recommendation at paragraph 8.26.

[180] Paragraph 7.17.

research programmes are directly related to the health of older people. Plainly DoH has strong claims for the role of coordinating department.

8.73. Nevertheless, although the choice is not an easy one, we believe that it is the Department of Trade and Industry, and under it the Office of Science and Technology, which should be responsible for the coordination of ageing related research. In this we agree with Help the Aged, which favours "the appointment of a 'champion for ageing research' in a central government department such as the Office of Science and Technology, to lead and direct a national research agenda on ageing."[181] OST already has responsibility for the research councils, and will therefore be aware of their virtues, and perhaps also of some of the failings which we have pinpointed. But a more important consideration is that the head of OST is the Government Chief Scientific Adviser (CSA). As such he is not, like other CSAs (or the Chief Medical Officer on DoH), responsible for only one department; he reports directly to the Prime Minister, and in that capacity can be regarded as being attached to the Cabinet Office.[182]

8.74. The ultimate responsibility must remain with the department, and its Ministers. OST will however need to set up a coordinating body to supply the necessary strategic direction. It should be possible for such a body to include representatives of all the major funders, public and private, without becoming "large and unwieldy".[183] This body should, unlike the Funders' Forum, meet several times a year at regular intervals; it should consult those involved in research on what they see as the most fruitful areas of research, and on what they regard as the gaps needing to be filled; it should take account of research being undertaken in other European countries and further afield (in particular in the United States and in Japan); and on this basis it should formulate and publish guidelines determining the direction to be taken by research. Thereafter it will monitor developments, review the activities of the research councils, call them to account for their activities, ensure that they are following the guidelines, review these periodically, and if necessary amend them. It will also be well placed to monitor research capacity for such an important topic, and to ensure that it is built up until it is adequate for the purpose.

8.75. We are not suggesting the setting up of a new non-departmental public body. The responsibility must remain that of DTI and OST, and of the CSA as head of OST. Moreover the scale of the problem does not warrant this. But the work of coordination will require allocation of sufficient funds for the infrastructure to enable this work to be carried out efficiently and in a manner which commands the confidence of the research community.

8.76. We mentioned earlier the creation of the National Cancer Research Institute (NCRI) as being a successful forum for collaboration between funders.[184] Professor Souhami said that "the creation of the National Cancer Research Institute has been one of the best things that the UK has done in terms of

---

[181] p 284.

[182] Until 1995 OST was itself part of the Cabinet Office. The arguments for and against it remaining part of DTI or reverting to the Cabinet Office were considered by the House of Commons Select Committee on Science and Technology (Fifth report, session 1999-2000, HC Paper 307-I, paragraph 127), and also by this Committee (*Science and Treaties*, Third Report, session 2003-04, HL Paper 110-I, paragraphs 412-417).

[183] RCUK's description of the Funders' Forum.

[184] Paragraph 8.49.

pulling together funding agencies around a common cause. What was really important there was that the Department of Health and the Government injected a small but sufficient amount of cash into the National Cancer Research Network and the National Translation Cancer Research Network to lubricate the research process and its translation into therapeutics. It was not a huge amount of money, £20 million or so a year, but it was incredibly important in terms of getting the whole structure going."(Q 500) It is moreover not a vastly greater sum than the £12 million already committed to be invested in the NDA.

8.77. Dr Goodwin agreed that the creation of a similar body would be the single best thing that could be done in the ageing research area. It seems to us that the NCRI is a model which should be carefully studied. It cannot be followed slavishly: ageing is a broader topic embracing a wider range of disciplines. But, with appropriate modification and adaptation, the NCRI represents the sort of body we have in mind. Professor Sally Davies seemed to agree: " … we are taking the opportunity to try to make all of the funders' for a—and this is no exception, the one for ageing—more effective … the model that has worked [is] the National Cancer Research Institute. That really has shown that, by bringing together the charities, the research councils, the Department of Health and everyone, they can map what the gaps are and be strategic."(Q 141)

8.78. We emphasise the limits of the responsibilities of DTI and OST. First, they will of course (like the Department for Health and Human Services and the NIA in the United States) have no control over how charities and other private funders allocate their funds; but they can and should have considerable influence. It must be in the interest of all concerned for there to be close collaboration between the work of the public and private sectors. Secondly, strategic direction and coordination does not involve the assessment of individual projects or of applications for research grants. Within the parameters of the strategic direction, these are matters which must remain the responsibility of the research councils, which are best qualified to undertake such assessments. And lastly, this is work which can and must be carried out without putting on researchers any additional bureaucratic burden. Consultation must not involve imposing any routine requirement for the provision of information. Those who wish to submit their views will of course be free to do so, but the inclusion on this body of a few senior and trusted members of the research community should be enough to ensure that it is kept informed of the main developments in the field.

8.79. Much of the success of such a body will depend on its being directed by a person who, while having the necessary authority for the purpose and commanding the confidence of the research community, has the time to devote to this task. The right person will be attracted to this post only if he or she believes that the direction of this body will have a major influence for good on ageing-related research in this country. Initially at least, this may need to be a full-time post. We do not believe that this can be an additional responsibility of the Director-General of Research Councils. His task is limited to the supervision of the research councils. He has responsibilities for their coordination with each other, but this might well conflict with the responsibility for coordinating their work with other departments, and with other public and private funders.

8.80. In formulating its strategic objectives, this body will need to bear in mind that the long-term goals of all research into ageing include the improvement of the health and well-being of people in this country and overseas, and support for the scientific community in this country and the economy of the country. We in no way wish to minimise the importance of "pure" scientific research, but even this cannot be conducted in a vacuum.

8.81. Among the first tasks of this body will be to carry out an audit of what is currently being undertaken in the field of ageing research, concentrating on projects which have ageing as their primary focus, or in which ageing is a secondary but nevertheless important factor. This should include projects financed by government departments, by the research councils and by the private sector. Without this basic information there can be no effective coordination.

8.82. Lastly and most importantly, among the main responsibilities of this body will be to supervise the training and career development of researchers in this field. Research into the scientific aspects of ageing in the UK can only thrive if the conditions are right for the best young researchers to be attracted to the subject, and to remain in this country to undertake the research.

8.83. **We conclude that the bodies currently responsible for the coordination of ageing-related research in the UK are not doing the job. The situation needs to be transformed. We believe however that this can be done without setting up a body modelled on the United States National Institute on Aging.**

8.84. **The responsibility for coordination must lie with the Department of Trade and Industry and the Office of Science and Technology. The Government's Chief Scientific Adviser will have an important part to play.**

8.85. **DTI and OST should set up a body with the membership, constitution, powers and funding necessary to provide the strategic oversight and direction of ageing-related research.**

8.86. **When deciding on the structure of this body, DTI and OST should learn from the successful structure of the National Cancer Research Institute.**

8.87. **Close collaboration with charities and private funders must be ensured by allowing them suitable representation.**

8.88. **There must be liaison with similar bodies in other countries, and developments in those countries must be taken into account.**

8.89. **Among the most important responsibilities of this body will be to promote research into ageing as a career for the best young researchers, and to supervise career development.**

CHAPTER 9: SUMMARY OF CONCLUSIONS AND RECOMMENDATIONS

9.1. In this chapter we summarise our conclusions and recommendations. The numbers in brackets refer to the relevant paragraphs in the text.

The devolved administrations

9.2. Some of our conclusions and recommendations to the Government relate to matters which, in Scotland, Wales and Northern Ireland, are within the competence of the devolved administrations. To this extent, our recommendations are not directly addressed to those administrations; but insofar as many of the facts on which they are based do not respect administrative boundaries, we hope that the devolved administrations too will consider implementing our recommendations with any necessary amendments and modifications. (1.11)

Demographic change

9.3. At current rates, life expectancy within the UK is increasing at the rate of about two years for each decade that passes. The consequences of this demographic change for all aspects of life are profound. As this Report will show, we have found little evidence that policy has been sufficiently informed by scientific understanding of the ageing process. (2.16)

9.4. We conclude that there is considerable uncertainty about whether healthy lifespan is increasing faster or slower than lifespan. The uncertainty comes from the variability in individual health trajectories through life, and the difficulty in applying objective measures of health and quality of life across different age groups. We believe that freedom from disability provides a more easily ascertainable objective measure of the quality of life. (2.29)

9.5. Further research should be undertaken to validate and apply appropriate measures to monitor the trends in healthy lifespan. We recommend that funds should be made available to the Office for National Statistics to enable it to carry out over a number of years the surveys needed to assess disability-free life expectancy. (2.30)

Promoting good health: physical activity

9.6. Local authorities can do much to help people of all ages, including older people, to benefit from exercise. Facilities for cycling are often poor or non-existent; sometimes even walking is a perilous activity. Local authorities should aim to improve facilities for exercise; they should make it their business to inform older people about these facilities; they should encourage them to use these facilities; and they should ensure that adequate transport is available. (3.25)

9.7. Exercise at all ages is one of the most effective ways to counter the adverse effects of ageing on functional capacity. The Government should publish plans showing how they intend to promote, in schools and elsewhere, the benefits of exercise as a factor contributing to improved health at all ages. (3.28)

9.8. Consent for the disposal of playing fields must be refused unless the facilities lost are to be replaced by sports or exercise facilities which are as good or better. (3.29)

Nutrition

9.9. Nutrition and oral health have major impacts on health throughout the lifespan. Since a person's health in old age reflects molecular and cellular damage that accumulates throughout life, and since nutrition affects the accumulation of such damage (adversely in the case of poor nutrition, beneficially in the case of good nutrition), the links between healthy eating and healthy ageing need to be better understood and communicated to the public. (3.36)

9.10. We welcome and commend the approach of the White Paper *Choosing Health*, and the importance it attaches to the provision of information about healthy nutrition. We recommend that this approach should be extended to cover the specific problems of older people. (3.37)

Individuality of the ageing process

9.11. In the light of improved knowledge of underlying biological mechanisms and the need to measure the efficacy of interventions aimed at improving healthy ageing, we recommend that specific attention be given to funding research on biomarkers of ageing. (3.47)

9.12. Most of the research on ageing and health within the UK is focused on specific diseases and medical conditions for which age is the single largest risk factor. However, there is little research on underpinning mechanisms of such diseases which may be linked to basic processes of ageing. The Department of Health and other medical research funders, including the major charities, should develop and implement strategies to address links between ageing and disease. (3.67)

Age-related diseases

9.13. Stroke is a major cause of long-term illness, disability and death, particularly among older people. Yet significant reductions in the long-term health consequences of a stroke can be made if very early assessments and treatments are provided, for example by locating scanners within accident and emergency departments. The Department of Health should make rapid treatment of stroke a priority. (4.12)

9.14. We recommend that the Government and research councils should, when allocating money to cancer research, place more emphasis on those cancers particularly prevalent among the elderly. We encourage Cancer Research UK to do likewise. (4.23)

Age-related disorders

9.15. We recommend that the Department of Health should continue to take urgent steps to remedy the shortage of dentists, and to encourage a habit of more frequent check-ups, especially among older people. (4.51)

9.16. Older people are disproportionately affected by many specific diseases and sensory impairments, and the expenditure directed at these diseases appears to be far lower than would be expected. A population with a growing number of older people will result in an increasing burden on society from some conditions for which age is a significant risk factor. (4.52)

9.17. The Government should re-examine their research priorities, and promote expenditure on research into the alleviation of those conditions which disproportionately affect older people. (4.53)

The built environment

9.18. The Office of the Deputy Prime Minister and the Department of Health should join with the Department for the Environment, Food and Rural Affairs and the Department of Trade and Industry in pressing ahead with the preparation of detailed plans for the elimination of deaths of older people caused by cold and damp, and should provide the resources to implement these plans. (5.11)

9.19. We urge the Government to take forward urgently the review of Part M of the Building Regulations, to bring up to date the Lifetime Home Standards, and to amend the Regulations to incorporate the revised standards. (5.15)

Transport

9.20. We recommend that, when reaching decisions on the review commissioned by the DVLA, the Department for Transport should not exclude the option of allowing licence-holders to determine for themselves the age at which they should cease to drive. (5.23)

9.21. We believe the evidence clearly shows how older people enter into a negative spiral towards dependency through social isolation and inactivity, often founded on lack of access to suitable transport, amenities and opportunities for exercise. (5.33)

9.22. Government, local authorities, transport companies and service providers should plan on the assumption that the average age of users and the proportion of older users will continue to increase. Compliance with regulations requiring provision for older people should be monitored. (5.34)

Communication

9.23. We believe that some of the most exciting opportunities for scientific advance to benefit older people arise through use of information technology. Industry self-regulation has notably failed to address these needs and opportunities. (5.39)

9.24. The Government's target should be that every home, including those in rural areas where social isolation of older people is often severe, should receive access to affordable high bandwidth IT connection within 3 years. If necessary, Ofcom should rely on its regulatory powers to secure this. Local authorities should offer older people training packages in the use of IT. (5.43)

Assistive technology

9.25. The Department of Health and the Office of the Deputy Prime Minister should make funds available to local authorities to set up the infrastructure needed for third generation social alarms. Local authorities should work closely with industry and with charities concerned with assistive technology in carrying this work forward. (5.58)

9.26. The Department of Health's investment in assistive technology should be extended to include technologies and devices that can assist in monitoring health conditions and detecting early signs of health problems by individuals in the home. (5.63)

Industry and commerce: the missed opportunity

9.27. The Government's policy of encouraging older people to remain in their homes as long as possible will be thwarted if industry does not respond to this challenge. (6.17)

9.28. The Government should consult with the Design Council, the Confederation of British Industry, the Institute of Directors, the Federation of Small Businesses, the British Chambers of Commerce, trade associations and trades unions on how they can best play an active part in developing these markets. (6.18)

9.29. Like the Foresight Ageing Population Panel, we encourage manufacturers and the finance and services sectors to seize this opportunity simultaneously to benefit their older customers and their shareholders. (6.19) ·

The National Service Framework

9.30. The Department of Health must set out clear and measurable standards for assessing the health of older people, with particular emphasis on the care and treatment of those diseases prevalent in old age. Claims that those standards have been met should not be made unless they are supported by hard evidence. (7.13)

9.31. We welcome the appointment of a "Government champion of older people". We believe that this must be a single minister of Cabinet rank who, whatever his or her title and departmental responsibilities, has full responsibility for bringing together and implementing all aspects of government policy relating to older people. (7.20)

Cost effectiveness

9.32. The initiation of studies of the cost-effectiveness of spending resources on prevention rather than treatment must be an important consideration for the Minister with overall responsibility for coordinating policy relating to older people. (7.28)

9.33. There must be effective supervision to ensure that it is the overall cost to the taxpayer which is considered, and not the cost to the budget of an individual department, to the NHS or to local government. (7.29)

Clinical records

9.34. The Department of Health and the NHS should consult with the scientific community as to how the data generated by the NHS could be improved, the regulatory framework simplified, and the bureaucracy reduced. (7.31)

Clinical trials

9.35. The Department of Health and the research councils should take steps to ensure that older people are not routinely excluded from clinical trials, and that positive steps are taken to include them in the testing of medicines to be used to treat conditions prevalent among older people. The Medicines and Healthcare Products Regulatory Agency should ensure that the pharmaceutical industry does likewise. (7.35)

Longitudinal studies

9.36. The Government should make additional funding available through the Department of Health and the research councils to implement joined-up programmes of longitudinal research on scientific aspects of ageing. (7.43)

Researchers

9.37. Multidisciplinary and translational clinical research, which is particularly important for ageing, has been hampered by the Universities Research Assessment Exercise. The Higher Education Funding Councils should, as a matter of urgency, consider how this problem can best be addressed in the forthcoming Research Assessment Exercise. (8.15)

Funding of research: the research councils

9.38. We recommend that the Economic and Social Research Council should urgently and significantly increase the proportion of its funding available for ageing-related research. The Director-General of Research Councils should supervise this. (8.29)

9.39. The research councils should ensure that when their scientific committees are considering applications for funding for ageing-related research, they include a majority of members with specific experience in these fields. (8.32)

Funding of research: the European Union

9.40. The Government must ensure that a very significant proportion of the resources allocated to the EU Seventh Framework Programme is set aside for ageing-related research. Members of the European Parliament should also press for this. (8.36)

Coordination of research

9.41. Our conclusion is that the attempts at coordination so far made under the aegis of the research councils are woefully inadequate. The image we have is of a series of ill-thought-out initiatives which have long titles, short lives, vague terms of reference, little infrastructure, and no sense of purpose. A radical reorganisation is essential. (8.58)

9.42. We conclude that the bodies currently responsible for the coordination of ageing-related research in the UK are not doing the job. The situation needs to be transformed. We believe however that this can be done without setting up a body modelled on the United States National Institute on Aging. (8.83)

9.43. The responsibility for coordination must lie with the Department of Trade and Industry and the Office of Science and Technology. The Government's Chief Scientific Adviser will have an important part to play. (8.84)

9.44. DTI and OST should set up a body with the membership, constitution, powers and funding necessary to provide the strategic oversight and direction of ageing-related research. (8.85)

9.45. When deciding on the structure of this body, DTI and OST should learn from the successful structure of the National Cancer Research Institute. (8.86)

9.46. Close collaboration with charities and private funders must be ensured by allowing them suitable representation. (8.87)

9.47. There must be liaison with similar bodies in other countries, and developments in those countries must be taken into account. (8.88)

9.48. Among the most important responsibilities of this body will be to promote research into ageing as a career for the best young researchers, and to supervise career development. (8.89)

APPENDIX 1: MEMBERS AND DECLARATIONS

Sub-Committee I

The members of the sub-committee which conducted this inquiry were:

§   Lord Broers

*†   Lord Drayson

*   Baroness Emerton

    Baroness Finlay of Llandaff

*   Baroness Hilton of Eggardon

*   Lord May of Oxford

    Lord Mitchell

*   Baroness Murphy

*   Lord Oxburgh

*   Lord Soulsby of Swaffham Prior

    Lord Sutherland of Houndwood (Chairman)

*   Lord Turnberg

*   Baroness Walmsley

§ Since 20 January 2005
* Co-opted
† Until 8 April 2005

Specialist Adviser

Professor Thomas Kirkwood, Professor of Medicine and Co-Director for the Institute for Ageing and Health at the University of Newcastle-upon-Tyne, was appointed as Specialist Adviser for the inquiry.

Declarations of Interest

Lord Drayson
> *Past Member of the BioIndustry Association and Chairman 2001-02.*
> *Founder and Ex CEO Powderject Pharmaceuticals plc 1993-2003.*
> *Chairman Oxford Children's Hospital Campaign.*
> *Chairman Entrepreneur in Residence at Said Business School, Oxford University.*

Baroness Emerton
> *Chairman, National Association of Hospital and Community Trusts.*
> *Director, Defence Medical Welfare Service.*

Baroness Finlay of Llandaff
> *Veliudre NHS Trust, Cardiff University and Marie Curie Cancer Care.*
> *President, Chartered Society of Physiotherapy.*

Baroness Murphy
> *Vice-President, Alzheimers Disease Society. Visiting Professor in Department of Psychiatry, Queen Mary University of London.*
> *Chairman , North East London Strategic Health Authority.*

Lord Soulsby of Swaffham Prior
> *President, Royal Institute of Public Health.*
> *Fellow of Academy of Medical Sciences.*

Lord Sutherland of Houndwood
> *Non-executive member of the board of NHP (property company whose main interest is care houses for the elderly).*

Lord Turnberg
> *Scientific Adviser, Association of Medical Research Charities.*
> *Vice-President, Academy of Medical Sciences.*
> *Ex-President, Royal College of Physicians.*

APPENDIX 2: LIST OF WITNESSES

The following witnesses gave evidence. Those marked * gave oral evidence.

Academy of Medical Sciences:

*   Professor Linda Partridge, Weldon Professor of Biometry, University College London

Age Concern England:

*   Dr Ian Nowell, Director for Innovation and Strategy

Alzheimer's Society:

*   Professor Clive Ballard, Director of Research

Arthritis Research Campaign:

*   Professor Cyrus Cooper, Professor of Rheumatology, University of Southampton

Biosciences Federation

Biotechnology and Biological Sciences Research Council:

*   Professor Linda Partridge, Weldon Professor of Biometry, University College London

Bone and Tooth Society

*   Mr Mike Brace, Chief Executive, Vision 2020

*   Professor Carol Brayne, Professor of Public Health Medicine, Cambridge University

British Geriatrics Society:

*   Professor Peter Crome, President-Elect

British Geriatrics Society (Scotland)

British Society for Research on Ageing:

*   Dr Richard Faragher

*   Professor Janet Lord, Chair

British Society of Gerontology:

*   Professor Chris Phillipson, President

Dr Simon Brownsell, Barnsley District General Hospital

Cancer Research UK:

*   Professor Robert Souhami, Director of Policy and Communication

Centre for Ageing and Public Health, London School of Hygiene and Tropical Medicine

Centre for Usable Home Technology (CUHTec):

         Dr Kevin Doughty, Consultant and Deputy Director

*   Mr Suresh Manandhar, Lecturer, Department of Computer Science, University of York

★   Professor Andrew Monk, Professor of Psychology, University of York

★   Professor John Robinson, Director of Research, Department of Electronics, University of York

★   Mr Peter Wright, Department of Computer Science, University of York

Dr John Clarkson, Director, Engineering Design Centre, Cambridge University

Professor Roger Coleman, Co-director, Helen Hamlyn Research Centre, Royal College of Art

Mr R Conrad

Dr Joanne Cook, University of Sheffield

Department for Transport:

★   Ms Charlotte Atkins MP, Parliamentary Under-Secretary of State

★   Ms Jan Brock, Head of the Drivers' Policy group, DVLA

★   Ms Yvonne Brown, Research Manager, Mobility Advice and Vehicle Information Service

★   Ms Ann Frye, Head of the Mobility and Exclusion Unit

Department of Health:

★   Dr Stephen Ladyman MP, Parliamentary Under-Secretary of State

★   Professor Sally Davies, Director of Research and Development

★   Ms Susan Lonsdale, Acting Head of the Policy Research Programme

★   Mr Craig Muir, Director, Older People and Disability Division

Department of Trade and Industry, OST:

★   Lord Sainsbury of Turville, Parliamentary Under-Secretary of State

★   Mr Paul Williams, Director, Research Councils Directorate

★   Mr Robert Diamond, Chief Executive, Diametric

Economic and Social Research Council:

★   Professor Ian Diamond, Chief Executive

Engineering and Physical Sciences Research Council:

★   Dr Alison Wall, Programme Manager, Infrastructure and Environment Programme

Mrs Dorothy Morgan Evans

Sir John Grimley Evans, Emeritus Professor of Clinical Geratology, Oxford University

★   Baroness Greengross, Executive Chair, International Longevity Centre UK

Professor M S Hawley, Barnsley District General Hospital

Help the Aged:

★   Dr James Goodwin, Head of Research

★   Mr Mervyn Kohler, Head of Public Affairs

Dr Alan Hipkiss, Institute of Gerontology, King's College London

INDEPENDENT Consortium

Institute of Gerontology, King's College London

International Longevity Centre UK

Professor Steve Jackson, Gurdon Institute, Cambridge University

Joseph Rowntree Foundation

★   Professor Elizabeth Kay, Manchester University Dental School, on behalf of the British Dental Association

★   Mrs Linda Kelly, Chief Executive, Parkinson's Disease Society, on behalf of the Parkinson's Disease Society

★   Professor Rose Anne Kenny, Professor of Cardiovascular Research, University of Newcastle Institute of Ageing and Health

Professor Peter Lansley, Professor of Construction Management, University of Reading

★   Professor Kennedy Lees, Professor of Cerebrovascular Medicine, University of Glasgow

★   Professor John Mathers, Professor of Human Nutrition, University of Newcastle, on behalf of the British Nutrition Foundation

Dr Claudine McCreadie, Research Fellow, Institute of Gerontology, King's College London

Medical Research Council:

★   Dr Diana Dunstan, Director of Research Management

Dr Frank Miskelly, Imperial College London

National Osteoporosis Society:

★   Professor Cyrus Cooper, Professor of Rheumatology, University of Southampton

Office for National Statistics

★   Professor Desmond O'Neill, Associate Professor in Medical Gerontology, Trinity College Dublin

★   Dr Roger Orpwood, Deputy Director, Bath Institute of Medical Engineering

Policy Research Institute on Ageing and Ethnicity

Dr Jane Preston, Institute of Gerontology, King's College London

QinetiQ

Queen Mother Research Centre for IT to support Older People

Professor Michael Rennie, Professor of Clinical Physiology, University of Nottingham

★   Professor Graham Russell, Norman Collisson Professor of Musculoskeletal Science, Oxford University

Research Councils UK

Royal Academy of Engineering:

*   Professor Garth Johnson, Professor of Rehabilitation Engineering, University of Newcastle

Royal College Physicians, Edinburgh

Royal Society

Royal Society of Edinburgh

Professor Aubrey Sheiham, Department of Epidemiology and Public Health, University College London

Society for Endocrinology

Mr Frederic Stansfield

*   Professor Karen Steel, Principal Investigator, Wellcome Trust Sanger Institute

Stroke Association:

*   Professor Peter Fentem, Chairman of Research and Development

Thomas Pocklington Trust

*   Professor Anthea Tinker, Professor of Social Gerontology, King's College London

Mr Peter Traynor, University of Sheffield

Dr Georgios Tsakos, Department of Epidemiology and Public Health, University College London

Tunstall Group Ltd:

*   Mr Kevin Alderson

*   Mr Steve Sadler, Technical Director

*   Dr Frans van der Ouderaa, Vice-President, Corporate Research, Unilever plc

Professor Alan Walker, University of Sheffield

Professor Robert Weale, Institute of Gerontology, King's College London

*   Professor Peter Weissberg, Medical Director and Professor of Cardiovascular Medicine, Cambridge University, on behalf of the British Heart Foundation

Wellcome Trust

Mr Gareth Williams

The following submitted papers which were not treated as formal evidence:

Felicia A Huppert

Alzheimer Scotland

Dr Nicholas Steel

APPENDIX 3: CALL FOR EVIDENCE

The House of Lords Select Committee on Science and Technology has appointed a Sub-Committee, chaired by Lord Sutherland of Houndwood, to inquire into the scientific aspects of ageing.

Average life expectancy in the UK is 77 years, and is still increasing. However, the healthy life expectancy in the UK stands at only 68 years, and the 2001 Census showed that half of the population aged over the statutory retirement age of 65 had a long-term illness or disability.

We therefore invite written evidence on how science and technology can help improve people's prospects of healthy and active life expectancy, and whether Government policy is in place to achieve this. In particular, we would welcome comments on:

The biological processes of ageing, including—

- What are promising avenues for research? How will such research benefit older people and delay the onset of long-term illnesses and disabilities?

- Differences between the sexes, and between different social and ethnic groups in the UK.

The application of research in technology and design to improve the quality of life of older people, including—

- Existing technologies which could be used to a greater extent to benefit older people;

- The development of new technologies.

In both of these areas—

- How effectively is research co-ordinated in the public, private and charitable sectors (including internationally)?

- Have the correct priorities been identified? Are there any gaps in research?

- Is there sufficient research capability in the UK?

- Is the research being used to inform policy?

Please note that the inquiry will not be considering health care for older people, or the economic aspects of the increase in the expectation of life, such as the future funding of pensions.

APPENDIX 4: NOTE OF THE SEMINAR

Present
Lord Drayson
Baroness Emerton
Baroness Hilton of Eggardon
Lord May of Oxford
Lord Mitchell
Baroness Murphy
Lord Oxburgh
Lord Soulsby of Swaffham Prior
Lord Sutherland of Houndwood (Chairman)
Lord Turnberg
Baroness Walmsley
Michael Collon (Clerk)
Dr Jonathan Radcliffe (Specialist Assistant)

Chairman
Professor Tom Kirkwood (Professor of Medicine, University of Newcastle, Specialist Adviser to the Sub-Committee)

Participants
Dr Alison Austin (Assistant Director, Office of Science and Technology, OST)
Steve Brown (BT – Martlesham Heath)
Professor Roger Coleman (Professor of Inclusive Design and Co-director of the Helen Hamlyn Research Centre at the Royal College of Art)
Professor David Cope (Parliamentary Office for Science and Technology)
Professor Peter Crome (President-elect, British Geriatrics Society)
Dr Deborah Dunn-Walters (British Society for Research on Ageing, BSRA)
Dr Diana Dunstan (Medical Research Council, MRC)
Doug Emery (Innovation Fellow, University of Sheffield)
Sir John Grimley Evans (Emeritus Professor of Clinical Geratology, Oxford University)
Dr James Goodwin (Head of Research, Help the Aged)
Ms Shabnam Khan (Economic and Social Research Council, ESRC)
Professor Steve Jackson (The Gurdon Institute, Cambridge University)
Professor Peter Lansley (Reading University)
Dr Lorna Layward (Research Manager, Help the Aged)
Mrs Mary Manning (Executive Director, Academy of Medical Sciences)
Dr Brian Merry (Liverpool University)
Dr Colin Miles (Biotechnology and Biological Sciences Research Council, BBSRC)
Ms Elizabeth Mills (former director, Research into Ageing)
Dr Helen Munn (Academy of Medical Sciences)

Dr Kedar Pandya (Engineering and Physical Sciences Research Council, EPSRC)

Professor Linda Partridge (University College London)

Martin Rumsey (Office of Science and Technology, OST)

Dr Jacob Sweiry (Wellcome Trust Science Funding Division)

Professor Alan Walker (Professor of Social Policy, University of Sheffield)

1. Professor Kirkwood opened the seminar, speaking on the timeliness of the inquiry, with an overview of ageing research in the UK.

2. A number of factors combined to make this an appropriate time for the inquiry: demographic changes, scientific progress, economic factors such as the cost of pensions and health care, rising expectations, and growing opportunities in an ageing world for exploiting the UK science base in age-related research.

3. The proportion of the global population aged 65 and over in 1900 was 1% (UK 5%); in 2000 it was 7% (UK 16%); and by 2050 it was estimated to be 20%, a figure the UK would reach in 2020. . Life expectancy continued to increase by about two years per decade. Translating this rate of increase into the immediate context, it meant that by the end of the seminar, for each hour of our life spans that would be used for this purpose, 12 minutes could be "recouped" through the ongoing increase in life expectancy.

4. From studies in Sweden, where statistics had been kept since 1860, it was clear that the maximum life-span, far from reaching a plateau, was accelerating.

5. Life expectancy was influenced by a number of factors. Genetic heritability accounted for about 25% of the differences between individuals. The ageing process was not genetically programmed, but was caused by an accumulation of cellular defects resulting from random molecular damage, with genes influencing cellular repair. Other factors affecting ageing were nutrition, lifestyle and environment. These were influenced by socio-economic factors, as could be seen from variations in life span recorded by different local authorities.

6. An important question concerned the relationship between intrinsic ageing and the development of age-related diseases such as osteoporosis, osteoarthritis and dementia.

7. A great deal of research was being carried out in the UK, sponsored mainly by charities, by the research councils, and by the EU. This was still fragmented, but some efforts at co-ordination had been undertaken by the Funders Forum for Research on Ageing, and recently by the National Collaboration on Ageing Research, which had been sponsored by several of the research councils. The challenges were that much of the science was new and poorly understood. There was a lack of clarity in the objectives, and in particular in the relationship between ageing and disease.

8. An example was established by Jeanne Calment, the longest-living person (122 years), who enjoyed good health through most of her life span. She retained a mischievous sense of humour as, in her words to a journalist in her later years, "I only ever had one wrinkle, and I am sitting on it".

9. Professor Steve Jackson discussed the biological determinants of ageing and longevity. He addressed what ageing was; why and how we aged; whether we could slow down or prevent ageing; and if so, whether this would be a good thing for society.

10. Ageing consisted of a loss of vigour; in skin, a loss of the subcutaneous fat cell layer leading to loss of suppleness and wrinkling; connective tissue changes; greying hair and loss of hair; impairment of the senses; osteoporosis; and cardiovascular and neurological degeneration. The underlying changes were cellular damage leading to impaired cell function; accumulated tissue and organ damage leading to dysfunction; and the loss of ability for tissue renewal.

11. Longevity, while influenced by the environment, was pre-ordained by genes. Identical twins tended to have similar life-spans. There were startling differences between species: people lived seven times longer than cats, which lived five times longer than mice, which in turn lived 25 times longer than fruit-flies. But selections for longer-lived laboratory animals revealed that certain mutations could dramatically increase life-span without apparent detrimental effects.

12. The rate of ageing was not fixed. The reason we had not evolved to live longer was that evolution acted to maximise reproductive success, so that there was little selective pressure to retain genes which might allow an individual to live significantly longer than its reproductive phase. On the contrary, evolution would select genetic factors which increased reproductive fitness even though this might cause accelerated ageing.

13. Oxidative stress was a major factor causing ageing, and a major target for oxidative damage was DNA. Laboratory animals selected to live longer were more resistant to oxidative stress. The reason calorie restriction enhanced the life-span of many organisms was related to its effects on oxidative metabolism and stress-resistance.

14. Most human cells could divide only a limited number of times, and when they reached the end of their replication capacity, they entered into senescence. There was evidence that cell senescence also took place during the ageing of a person. Telomeres in cells provided a cell-division clock: when they became too short, senescence was induced. There were strong links to DNA damage. Another link to DNA damage was Werner's syndrome, an autosomal recessive disorder which led to death in the fourth to sixth decade of life.

15. In principle, it was possible that damaged DNA could be better repaired, rates of cell death reduced, and hence ageing slowed down, using drugs, but this led to the questions whether extending human life-span was desirable for the individual or for society.

16. Ageing research was not an isolated discipline, but was closely connected to research into diseases such as Alzheimer's, Parkinson's, cancer and cardiovascular diseases.

17. Sir John Grimley Evans spoke about the impacts of ageing on human health, and the prospects for science-based intervention.

18. Biologically, ageing was characterised by a loss of adaptability manifested in age-specific mortality rates. Between birth and age 10, mortality rates decreased with age, but from age 11 onwards they increased. For effective prevention of late-life disability ageing had to be seen as a life-long process, with some determinants of late life trajectory acting in childhood and in utero. Biological ageing was the result of interaction between intrinsic (genetic) and extrinsic (environmental and lifestyle) factors, but was modulated by non-ageing effects: selective survival, cohort effects such as education, and the differential challenge exemplified in the many aspects of cultural ageism.

19. Science wanted to know why ageing came about, but there were two sorts of questions relating to causes and to mechanisms. Epidemiology sought causes, but needed biological, physiological and social sciences to elucidate mechanisms. In coping with human ills it was possible to remove causes or to interrupt mechanisms. Neither approach was generally better than the other.

20. In the UK, medical, social and biological geratology had followed separate traditions; the time had come to try in particular to bring medical and biological developments closer together. The impediments included different career structures and funding sources, and difficulties in extrapolating from the short-lived animals studied by biologists to the human being. Developments in molecular biology had now made such extrapolation more reliable. The focus of biologists on longevity contrasted with the medical concern with disability. There was a need for greater complementarity between the work of the three traditions of geratology.

21. There was a divergence between projected rates of disability and the rates found in practice. In a US study of the period 1982 to 2001, it had been expected that the numbers of people over age 65 who were disabled would increase steadily over time as life expectancy was lengthened. In fact, in the US there were now 2 million fewer older people with disability than would have been expected if disability rates of 1982 had continued. The trend was "live longer, die faster".

22. There was thus encouraging evidence that the present pattern of age-associated disability could be improved. Age-associated loss of adaptability meant that the older one was when first suffering potentially disabling disease (such as heart attack or stroke), the more likely one was to die rather than linger with disability. This was the principle of "postponement as prevention". Disability arose when there was an "ecological gap" between what an individual needed or reasonably wished to do and what his or her environment required for this to be achieved. Technological approaches could improve a person's range of function and reduce the demands of the environment. There were problems associated with the development and deployment of technological approaches to the prevention and management of disability. Areas of particular need included technologies to help people with cognitive impairment and those suffering trauma or undergoing surgery.

23. In *discussion* of these topics a number of points were raised.

24. Lord Turnberg asked about the relation between genes and environment. Matters such as status in society and marital status affected longevity. Sir John Grimley Evans agreed that there was a relationship, but it was complex. It was clear from US studies that education was highly significant. It gave the ability to earn more and to control the pace of working; educated persons were better able to respond to progress in scientific knowledge, and to balance present pleasure against future happiness.

25. Lord Sutherland asked why it was necessary to make a distinction between ageing and disease, and wondered if this was caused only by the structure of research. Professor Kirkwood said that there was agreement on the need for research to combat disease, but not on the need for research to combat ageing, as had become clear when Alzheimer's was classified as a disease. It was more difficult to raise funding for research into ageing. Dr Goodwin agreed that the pragmatic distinction did affect fundraising from donors and the general public. Dr Dunstan said that the MRC was concerned only with the quality of research.

26. There was general agreement on the lack of dialogue between medical and biological researchers. It occurred in all areas, but was pronounced in gerontology. Lord Oxburgh pointed out that the design of the Norman Foster building at Imperial College encouraged interaction between the disciplines.

27. Professor Lansley thought it was easier for researchers to focus on diseases. Professor Partridge said that attempts were made to focus on basic biology (diet and health) rather than specific diseases. The increased understanding of biological interventions had led to an explosion of research. Dr Dunn-Walters said that the three research societies had carved up the research territory and moved further apart. The BSRA welcomed medical researchers, but they were not keen to join. Medical and biological researchers were pulled apart by the imperatives of their jobs.

28. Professor Peter Lansley introduced the topic of better environments for healthy ageing.

29. The EPSRC supported the EQUAL Initiative, aimed at Extending the Quality of Life. It was concerned with creating better home environments (adapting buildings for older people); creating better hospital environments (using colour coding to facilitate use by older people, and colour and lighting to promote recovery and well-being); creating better urban environments (e.g. by designing dementia friendly streets); and creating better consumer products.

30. The EQUAL Initiative had started in 1997, since when it had spent £8.6m funding 48 research teams in 33 universities. It was multidisciplinary, bringing together scientists concerned with the physical sciences, design and engineering with those involved with social, health and medical research. They designed new technologies for use in existing homes, in shops, and in transport, and promoted new approaches for designing better environments and products. These reduced the effects of physical impairment, vision and hearing loss, dementia and other cognitive impairment.

31. There was practical evidence of the value of this research, which was designed to be close to the end user rather than an academic talking shop. Of the contacts of the EQUAL Network, which supported dissemination of the findings from the EQUAL Initiative, only one third were researchers; one third were professionals and practitioners, the remainder older and disabled people. In the words on one of these, "Leading-edge of research meets sharp-end of practice tempered by the realities of ageing and disability".

32. Lately however support for research had been tailing off. There was little political support, and it was not even clear which government department had responsibility.

33. Steve Brown looked at design and assistive technology for older people.

34. Telecare was the use of information and communication technology (ICT) to support independent living for older, frail and disabled people. The existing first generation telecare systems were community alarm systems, such as pull-cords and pendants linked to auto-dialling phones. The technology was proven; it was low cost, and used by all local authorities. It was non-invasive, requiring the client to initiate an alarm and alert a remote carer.

35. The second generation consisted of emerging telecare systems; "smart systems" incorporating "smart sensors". These were capable of alerting a carer when the client was disabled, and could incorporate safety and security applications, but they were still based on response to an alarm, though in this case

an alarm created by the system rather than the client. They were invasive, monitoring people in their own homes. They were currently being trialled by local authorities.

36. Finally, future third generation telecare systems involved highly complex data processing and novel sensors, designed not to react to events but to prevent them occurring. They were still at the design stage, but with some early trials. They were designed to be used in conjunction with first and second stage telecare.

37. Professor Alan Walker explained the work of the Research Councils.

38. Four of the Research Councils (MRC, ESRC, EPSRC, BBSRC) all sponsored major research programmes or portfolios relevant to ageing. One of the most important of these was the ESRC Growing Older programme, launched in 1999 and the largest social sciences research programme on ageing ever mounted in the UK.

39. In 2001 these four Research Councils set up the UK National Collaboration on Ageing Research (NCAR) to stimulate inter-disciplinary research and develop a new cross-Council approach to ageing research. A broader overview of ageing research was maintained by the Funders Forum for Research on Ageing, which brought together the four Research Councils, six leading charities, the OST and the Department of Health. The NCAR was responsible for creating the European Forum on Population Ageing Research. It was also leading ERA-AGE, a European Union initiative coordinating research into ageing in nine EU countries. UK research, while behind the US in terms of coordination and strategic thinking, was the leader in Europe.

40. "New Dynamics of Ageing" was a cross-Research Council initiative launched in 2004, and the largest UK programme of interdisciplinary research on ageing to date. Among its aims were to ensure that science fed into policy and practice, to cross the boundaries of disciplines, and to bring young scientists into the topic. It was looking at ageing across the whole lifespan, and not just among older people.

41. In summary, the Research Councils working in partnership were coordinating different scientific approaches, stimulating inter-disciplinary research, leading Europe, increasing investment in research, and bridging the gap between research and policy.

42. Dr James Goodwin discussed research by charities.

43. Help the Aged was a leading member of the Association of Medical Research Charities (AMRC) which brought together 112 members to provide guidance on research governance, ethics, policies and processes. In 2002/03 £660m had been spent on biomedical research, £578m by the top five members. A very large proportion of this involved research into diseases which were prevalent among the elderly. There were an increasing number of applications for funding, 19 out of 20 of which had to be refused. However there were only six charities in the Funders Forum on Ageing Research, four of which supported ageing research in science and technology areas.

44. An international comparison across the four UN regions revealed three strategic problems applicable to the UK: low relative investment; fragmentation and lack of capacity; and absence of strategic direction. The European Union approach was particularly disappointing; ageing research was a low priority. In 2002 expenditure on research into ageing in the UK was considerably higher than in the whole of the rest of the EU. The EU Sixth Framework Programme made only limited reference to ageing as a priority. In the USA, by contrast, the National

Institute of Aging combined high order strategic organisation with enviable levels of funding; this paradigm should be considered by the Committee.

45. In summary, there were a number of matters the Committee should consider. There were numerous biomedical charities with age-related disease well represented, but few entirely dedicated to ageing research. The comparative expenditure on ageing was moderate, but quality assurance mechanisms ensured that it had a high impact. The priorities went beyond funding: charities were well placed to work with Government to increase funding levels, improve strategic direction, and maximise the benefits of new research.

46. In subsequent *discussion* the following points were made.

47. Professor Kirkwood stressed that an issue for the Committee would be how far an inquiry into scientific aspects of ageing could extend into questions of disability. Professor Coleman thought disability was largely created by the impact of the environment on ageing. Lord Sutherland said that the Committee should concentrate on how different contexts affected disability.

48. Professor Lansley said that the EQUAL Initiative provided strong evidence of the return of investment in the new technologies. A cost/benefit analysis must involve economists and business schools. Professor Kirkwood instanced the large benefits derived by the NHS from a minimal investment in ensuring that the elderly were provided with walking sticks of the right length.

49. In relation to third generation assistive technology, Lord Oxburgh asked why individuals were reluctant to wear devices. Mr Brown said the reason was not known; there had been no research into what older people wanted.

50. Professor Kirkwood suggested that there was a need to look at the differences between the sexes, and between different social and ethnic groups. Dr Sweiry, agreeing, said that the Biobank Project, funded jointly by the Wellcome Trust, the MRC and the Department of Health, would provide enormous quantities of data to assist in uncovering genetic and environmental factors affecting ageing and leading to diseases prevalent among the elderly. Professor Walker agreed with Baroness Walmsley that there was not enough research into the cultural aspects of ageing. However there was a huge database, and the ESRC was a significant investor, for example through the Growing Older programme.

51. Discussion turned to the direction and funding of research. Lord Sutherland said that the Treasury regarded young people as producers, but the elderly only as consumers, which might be a reason why research tended to focus on infants and the young. He asked how effective it was to attempt to drive research strategies by targeted calls for grant applications in particular areas. Professor Partridge explained that the National Institute for Aging in Washington DC regularly invited research proposals on specific topics. Lord May thought there was scope for programmes calling for responses in particular areas provided these were chosen by people with the right attitudes.

52. Professor Kirkwood wondered why the Department of Health was not represented at the seminar, and whether they were put off by the word "scientific" in the title of the inquiry. Lord Sutherland thought that there was a radical divide in the Department between research and its application. For them the vital question seemed to be, not whether research would reduce expenditure generally, but whose budget was affected? Was the benefit going to accrue to the body whose budget bore the cost of the research?

53. Lord Sutherland concluded by thanking all those who had attended the seminar, and in particular those who had made presentations, for their contributions to a very valuable debate. It would be of great assistance in focusing the work of the inquiry.

APPENDIX 5: NOTE OF THE VISIT TO WASHINGTON DC

54. The Sub-Committee visited Washington DC, Bethesda and Baltimore on 18 and 19 January 2005. Members present were Lord Oxburgh, Lord Sutherland of Houndwood (Chairman), Lord Soulsby of Swaffham Prior and Baroness Walmsley. They were supported by Michael Collon (Committee Clerk), Jonathan Radcliffe (Specialist Assistant) and Michael Norman (Committee administrator). They were accompanied by staff of the British Embassy: Phil Budden (First Secretary, Science and Technology), Joshua Mandel (Senior Adviser, Science and Technology) and Matt Bricken (Research Assistant, Global Issues Group).

55. The purpose of the visit was to study the organisation and conduct in the United States of research into matters related to ageing, both publicly and privately funded, and to hear about some of the research projects being undertaken.

Ellison Medical Foundation

56. The Committee first visited the Ellison Medical Foundation. The Foundation was established as a non-profit corporation in the latter part of 1997 through the generosity of Lawrence J. Ellison, founder and CEO of Oracle, "for the purpose of positively affecting scientific discovery by funding basic biological and biomedical research, with the expectation that the research would significantly impact people's lives".

57. A Scientific Advisory Board was established in 1998 to guide the Foundation in the fields of research that would benefit from financial support and have an important impact on public health. The Foundation initially focused on funding research that addressed the basic biological components of ageing, including its processes, related diseases and disabilities. The first awards on ageing research were presented in 1998.

58. The Committee met Dr Richard Sprott. Dr Sprott was previously the Associate Director of the National Institute on Aging, but in 1998 was recruited to become the first Executive Director of the Ellison Medical Foundation.

59. Dr Sprott told the Committee that Mr Ellison had taken the view that public funding of research was too much orientated towards research into diseases, to the exclusion of basic scientific research. He felt that public funds allocated to research by the National Institutes of Health (NIH), and in particular the National Institute on Aging (NIA), did not allow for sufficiently high risk research to be carried out. He was content himself to take risks with his own money, and to fund twenty projects even if it was likely that only one of them would be successful.

60. New Scholar awards of $50,000 a year for 4 years were made to young researchers for the sort of creative research for which they would not get public funds. The funding was for good people with good ideas, rather than for projects. Applications were limited to 4 pages, though a number of referees were required. A small outside review group decided which applications should succeed.

61. A number of Senior Scholar awards were also made each year, consisting of grants of $150,000 a year for 4 years made to established researchers, together with grants of the same order for administration costs. The total value of Senior Scholar awards was therefore of the order of $1 million. Applications for these were only 2 pages long. They went before a panel of 6 reviewers who read all the applications and listed the top 6 in order of priority. Applications listed by all the

reviewers were automatically granted; those listed by none were automatically refused. Those whose applications were listed by some but not all reviewers might be asked to make a further 3-page application.

62. On the basis of such brief applications, the Foundation had been putting $20 million a year into aging research. It would not be possible for public funds to be allocated on the basis of such a process. The Chairman contrasted this with the position in the UK, where researchers spent a substantial proportion of their time completing applications for grants.

63. Dr Sprott explained that only 4% of the funds were spent on administration. The work depended entirely on the will of the benefactor. It was open to Mr Ellison at any time to review the direction of the funding, and to terminate projects. He and the Scientific Advisory Board had recently independently reached the conclusion that funding work on infectious diseases was not worth continuing, and that more funds should be put into ageing research.

64. The Foundation drew a sharp distinction between the biology of ageing and diseases of ageing. Its funds were applied to basic biology, not to cures for diseases or, for example, to vaccines. Its objective was not extension of life expectancy, but improving the quality of the terminal third of the lifespan. Its interest was in understanding the basic processes of ageing. Until recently the Foundation had contributed 20% of the funds spent on basic research into ageing; now the NIA was contributing more, but the proportion funded by the Foundation was still 10%.

65. As an example of work currently funded, Dr Sprott gave an outline of the work on cell senescence and the shortening of telomeres. $20 million spent on this was well worthwhile.

66. Internationally, in the 1980s, investments in ageing research had been made by the UK, France, Italy and the Netherlands. After putting a great deal of money into the field over 5 years, France and the Netherlands had decided that this work was unproductive, and ceased to fund it. But Italy had persevered with the education of new scientists in basic molecular science.

67. The key was to attract the brightest young scientists and direct them towards pure research into ageing. The effect was that after 4 years they were committed to this research, which resulted in some of the best young scientists being in this field. This raised the profile of ageing research, which in turn attracted the best scientists. Until a few years previously ageing had, apart from nutrition, been the least highly regarded field of research. The position now was very different.

68. The Foundation was not afraid of controversy. Much of the work it funded involved experiments on animals, and it might soon consider funding stem cell research.

69. Funding was also provided for conferences and developing infrastructure. For example, the Foundation supported the "Science of Aging Knowledge Environment" (SAGE KE)—an online resource for researchers hosted by the American Association for the Advancement of Science.

70. Asked how the position in the UK might be improved, Dr Sprott said that he did not see any value in a bricks and mortar institute dedicated solely to ageing research; this tended to isolate researchers on ageing from other researchers. The UK could have great influence on sharply focussed basic research with an investment of $20 million. The problem was to get the best scientists to leave

existing posts in other institutions. A measure of success was whether the work achieved what the application for the funding grant had said hoped to be achieved.

71. It was noted that in the US, not many researchers were medically qualified. Dr Sprott was not convinced that research carried out by MDs was of particularly high quality.

National Institute on Aging, Washington DC

72. The Committee next visited the headquarters of the National Institute on Aging (NIA). The NIA is one of the 27 institutes of the National Institutes of Health (NIH) based in the Washington suburb of Bethesda. Congress granted the authority for the setting up of the institute in 1974. The purpose is to provide leadership in ageing research, training, health information dissemination, and other programmes relevant to ageing and older people. Subsequent amendments designated the NIA as the primary federal agency on Alzheimer's disease research.

73. The NIA sponsors research on ageing through extramural and intramural programmes. The extramural programme funds research and training at universities, hospitals, medical centres, and other public and private organisations nationwide. The intramural program conducts basic and clinical research on the NIH campus in Bethesda, and in Baltimore.

74. Over lunch, the Committee met Dr John Hardy, Chief of the Laboratory of Neurogenics, and were shown around his laboratory. Originally from the UK, he had moved to the US in the 1990s. He still retained close ties with British academe, and had recruited several researchers from research groups in the UK. Dr Hardy felt that the UK had become over-restrictive in its regulation of human tissue samples; it was increasingly difficult to obtain specimens for research. It was his opinion that stem cell research would not benefit his particular field.

75. The Committee met Dr Richard J. Hodes, the Director of the NIA; Dr Huber Warner, associate director with responsibility for the Biology of Aging Program; Dr Miriam Kelty, associate director for Extramural Affairs; Dr John Haaga, deputy associate director of the Behavioral and Social Research Program; and Dr Tamara Jones.

76. Dr Hodes explained that there had been considerable resistance to the setting up of the NIA, including two Presidential vetoes. However it now had an annual budget of $1billion. It had a considerable intramural research facility, but most of the funds went on extramural research. There were four extramural research programmes:

- the Biology of Aging Program, headed by Dr Warner;

- the Behavioral and Social Research Program;

- the Neuroscience and Neuropsychology Program; and

- the Geriatrics and Clinical Gerontology Program.

77. The primary task of the NIA was the funding and supervision of research projects in each of these four programmes. A distinction was drawn between research into the ageing process, the impact of the process on individual diseases especially prevalent among older people, and research on those diseases. It was easier to fund research into specific diseases than research into the ageing process.

78. Asked about the accountability of the NIA, Dr Hodes said it was responsible to Congress for the use of the funds voted for it. The mission of the Institute was

very broad, and the appropriation came with little specificity as to the use to be made of it. However the legislation establishing the NIA had been amended to designate the NIA as the primary Federal agency for Alzheimer's disease research, and it was expected that at least half the NIA budget would be spent on research into Alzheimer's.

79. There was no requirement to provide an annual report to Congress, or to the Department of Health and Human Services (DHHS). There could however be Congressional hearings; normally these were for the purposes of information, but they could occasionally become confrontational.

80. Dr Jones added that in 2004 the NIA had attended a record of nine hearings on, inter alia, appropriation, Alzheimer's, longevity, frailty, retirement, the Older Americans Program 2004, and meals on wheels. The House of Representatives had done away with its committee on aging, but the Senate had two committees with interests in the topic. The NIA was not allowed to lobby Congress, but there was a daily process of contact, and regular provision of information.

81. Continuing, Dr Hodes said that accountability for the quality of NIA research was ultimately to the National Advisory Council on Aging (NACA), which advised the Secretary of the DHHS, the Assistant Secretary for Health, the Director of the NIH, and himself as Director of the NIA. The Council met three times a year to consider applications for research and training, and to recommend funding for those applications that showed promise of making valuable contributions. The Council also made recommendations to the Director of the NIA regarding research conducted at the Institute. There was a simple test for success: had research improved the quality of life of older people?

82. Dr Hodes said that the NIA did not have a great deal of contact with the Ellison medical foundation. Each was aware of and respected the other's work, but the Foundation's work was almost entirely concentrated on young researchers. Dr Warner added that they had to be careful to avoid overlap with funding of research by private foundations. There was not yet much overlap in the field of ageing because there was not much such research. However nearly every Ellison senior scholar was also funded by the NIA. He was more worried about the balance between programmes than about overlap.

83. Dr Kelty explained that the scientific community trusted the NIA because research grants were not made by policy-makers, while the reason administrators trusted the allocation of research funds by the NIA was because peer review demonstrated that the research was of value.

84. An example of a project to which large funds had been allocated was biomarkers. Fifteen years earlier, the Biology of Aging Program had set aside funds for research into biomarkers, but ultimately it had not proved useful. The research had been attempting to find predictive indications of ageing, but the technology was not ready for it.

85. Dr Warner said that a contrast was the programme on the genetic and molecular basis of ageing. The first five years had not proved promising, but they had persevered, and the second five years had been spectacular. Research based on fruit flies had shown that selecting the offspring of older mothers for two or more generations could lead to an increase in life expectancy of up to 75%. A number of scientists working on different but interrelated aspects of this had had relatively little contact, and the NIA initiative had brought them all together.

86. Dr Haaga spoke about demographic issues. The Behavioral and Social Research Program had made a number of grants on work designed to measure objectively people's fundamental well-being. Measurement of healthy life expectancy (HLE) was a hot area of research. In the US, unlike the UK, HLE had been rising at the same rate as life expectancy over previous years, but currently obesity had the potential to reverse this.

87. Asked what datasets the UK should start building now as a basis for future research, Dr Haaga explained that the health care system in the UK provided a single database which facilitated research. In the US, by contrast, there were problems about access to Medicare data and medical records. They had now brokered access to that information, and to information about income for research on the social aspects. But, as in the UK, there was more concern about protecting privacy, at the expense of making data available for research.

88. One of the most profound discoveries of the last 50 years had been the impact of social status on health. This dwarfed differences between the sexes. Much of the data had come from the Baltimore longitudinal study. This had been going for forty or fifty years. Subjects came back every year for two days of tests. The results were good, but the study was expensive. Data from other countries where health statistics were well documented were also used. Dr Haaga cited the 2002 English Longitudinal Study of Ageing.

89. The US had no tolerance for discrimination by age, and would not countenance the NHS view that a person could be too old for treatment to be cost-effective and worthwhile. But there was considerable discrimination by social status.

90. The Chairman explained that the Committee had concerns about the disparate nature of research activity in the UK, and the apparent lack of coordination. Dr Hodes agreed that there were also coordination problems in the US, both between all the institutes comprised in the National Institutes of Health, and also with other researchers looking at different parts of the life-span, including child health.

91. Training was an important part of the NIA's work: not only training researchers for such projects, but also training those to support research. They were at that time training an outstanding economist to work on the ageing process. Dr Haaga explained that, although there were country-wide variations, there was a general shortage of gerontologists, and of nurses with specific training in gerontology. The NIA was funding programmes to insinuate gerontology into the training programmes of all medical staff.

92. Asked what he felt were promising long-term areas of research, Dr Warner instanced research into the replacement of cells—possibly but not necessarily stem cell research. The most important thing the Biology of Aging Program could do was increase the mobility of over-70s. Dr Haaga suggested that it was important to persuade people to do what was good for them, rather than just lecturing them about it.

Fogarty International Center

93. The Committee briefly visited the Fogarty International Center, the smallest of the NIH institutes, which supported the NIH through international partnerships and addressed global health challenges through collaborative research and training programmes. The Director explained the international work of the NIH.

National Institute on Aging Intramural Research Program, Baltimore

94. On Wednesday 19 January the Committee visited the NIA Intramural Research Program in Baltimore. The Committee met Dr Michele Evans, Deputy Scientific Director of the NIA; Dr Vilhelm Bohr, Chief of the Laboratory of Molecular Gerontology; Dr David Schlessinger, Chief of the Laboratory of Genetics; Dr Donald Ingram, Acting Chief of the Laboratory of Experimental Gerontology; Dr Linda Fried, Director of the Division of Geriatric Medicine and Gerontology at Johns Hopkins Hospital (who is also a member of the National Advisory Council on Aging); and Dr Mark Mattson, Chief of the Laboratory of Neurosciences.

95. The Committee was welcomed by Dr Michele Evans.

96. Dr Will Bohr explained that he was also a professor at Aarhus University and had worked in Europe, so that he was in a good position to compare funding in the US and in Europe. Only 10% of the NIA research budget funded intramural research; the remaining 90% funded extramural research. This could be and was used to fund research in other countries. This was in contrast to EU funding, which could be used only to fund research in the Member States.

97. Dr Bohr was strongly of the view that a research centre was necessary. A virtual centre was inadequate. A real centre with walls had the advantages of being able to attract top-quality research scientists by paying them competitive salaries. It provided a training ground for new researchers, and created a good working environment.

98. Molecular biology of ageing was now top-tier science. The goal was to add life to years, rather than years to life. The laboratory did not attempt to cover the whole subject, but focused on those areas at the cutting edge at molecular level. He thought that the NIA attempted to cover too much ground, and suggested that if the UK set up a national research institute, it should not have too wide a remit, but should concentrate on a small number of matters specific to ageing. The advantage of an intramural programme was that it had the resources for high-cost research like the Baltimore longitudinal study. In the past, the programme had dealt with high-risk research which could not be done privately. Now however the NIA had to compete with other researchers.

99. Dr Bohr saw environmental effects as being at least as important as genetics on ageing. However, there were some rare genetic diseases that allowed scientists to understand the ageing process, especially Werner's syndrome, which led to premature ageing, and Bloom's syndrome, sufferers of which had a much higher incidence of cancer. The effects of low-level radiation were also being studied. His view in general was that some environmental stress was beneficial, as it conditioned the body.

100. Dr Evans was asked about the relationship between the intramural and extramural research programmes. She replied that there was discussion between the two, but that traffic was mainly one-way. The intramural programme had more latitude to get people to work on long-term research which did not necessarily look as if it might have an immediate impact on ageing. An example was Dr Schlessinger's work on genetics. When the laboratory was set up 5 years ago, its major impact on ageing could not have been predicted.

101. The intramural programme obtained resources without competing for them, and was held accountable mainly through informal peer review. Its programme was often adjusted in the light of external evaluation. It was possible to tell

researchers about a change in direction, and easy to recruit any necessary new researchers; but less easy to dispense with those no longer necessary.

102. Asked what the critical mass might be for a similar establishment in the UK, Dr Evans replied that it would not have to be as large as the NIA. Work could be done with fewer researchers, but would have to be restricted to fewer topics. Examples might be 5 years on molecular biology, followed by 5 years on translational work. It was a question of picking out the key areas scientists would want to work in. The work might be done in partnership with UK universities. University researchers had the advantage of being able to contact researchers in pharmaceutical companies; NIA researchers were not allowed any such contact.

103. Dr David Schlessinger gave an overview of the work on Genetics. His field of statistical genetics, which lay between epidemiology and pure genetics, was a relative newcomer to gerontological research. His work looked at multiple causality, trying to distinguish the effects of specific genes. The laboratory was studying the extent to which phenomena previously associated solely with ageing might have genetic origins. An example was the menopause. This occurred at about age 50 in most women of whatever ethnic group. However in the case of 3% it occurred in the low 30s or early 40s. This had found to be for genetic reasons: they were born with too few oocytes to enable them to support a full reproductive life-span. For them the menopause, though age-related, was determined at birth.

104. The Committee was told that geneticists were critical of the UK biobank because the level of self-reporting was too high. Many genetic studies had been carried out in Sardinia. The founder population had all arrived at about the same time, and until recently there had been little inter-marriage with other groups. Studies had taken place in four towns among people who had themselves, their parents and grandparents all been born there.

105. Dr Donald Ingram explained that the Laboratory of Experimental gerontology was the newest arrival at the NIA. Current experiments included animal modelling; attempting to identify genes with effects on ageing; cognitive enhancements which might have a direct effect on Alzheimer's; and nutrition and the effect of calorie restriction. This was monitored by the Aging Intervention Testing Program (AITP), and there had been requests for access to it from all over the world.

106. Dr Ingram was critical of advertisements for dietary supplements and hormone replacement therapies which promoted their ability to increase longevity. They had no basis in fact. He felt that regulations were lax in the case of natural ingredients.

107. Dr Linda Fried gave an overview of the work at Johns Hopkins University. They had fifty researchers working solely on ageing. This required a different mindset and different financing to single researchers working on single projects. The work was focused on frailty, seeking to answer why older people became frail. This needed a multi-disciplinary team. The university's work also gave high priority to training, and to translating research into public health practice.

108. Dr Fried said that if a topic excited colleagues, they would want to work together to get funding for it. An alternative was where in the case of a number of related projects the whole could be said to be greater than the sum of the parts. Usually a number of related projects were funded from different sources. It was not essential for all the projects to be funded from the same source, but it was helpful.

109. There was a need to articulate the benefits of an ageing population. Society had abandoned the notion that the elders were the natural governors. This needed to be reconsidered. The use of the experience and wisdom of older people was good socially and good for their own health, and it enabled them to feel they were putting something back into the community. Age cut-offs were arbitrary, and there should be more flexible ways of culling older people. We should not throw away the investment in the education of 20% of the population; the academic world in particular was not making use of their knowledge and experience.

110. Dr Mark Mattson gave an outline of the work of the Laboratory of Neurosciences on Alzheimer's, Parkinson's and Huntingdon's diseases, and of his work on calorie restriction. It was now clear that overeating had a major impact on cardiovascular disease, diabetes, stroke and some cancers—and possibly also Alzheimer's and Parkinson's. Experiments with rats and monkeys had shown that calorie restriction led to increased lifespan. Rats on restrictive diets lived 30% longer, and showed the effects of improved memory. However, there were questions over whether the artificial experimental conditions gave a real control group against which to compare the effects. A pilot calorie restriction experiment was underway with human volunteers, though still in the preliminary stages.

111. Asked about the distinction between ageing and age-related diseases, Dr Mattson said that it had at one time been his opinion that there was no such distinction, and that the two were interrelated, but this was no longer his view. It was not the case that we would all get Alzheimer's if only we lived long enough.

Acknowledgement

112. In addition to those to whom we have specifically referred, the Committee met a large number of other people on this visit. All were extremely welcoming, helpful and generous with their time. We thank them all. We especially thank Dr Sprott, Dr Bohr, Dr Jones and the Embassy staff for their work in arranging our visit.

APPENDIX 6: ABBREVIATIONS AND ACRONYMS USED IN THIS REPORT

Abbreviations

Foresight	A programme launched in 1993, and now run by OST. Panels look at what might happen in the future in particular fields. The report of the Foresight Ageing Population Panel, *The Age Shift – Priorities for Action* was published by DTI in December 2000.
Funders' Forum	A body bringing together those responsible for funding research on specific topics, e.g. the Funders' Forum for Research on Ageing and Older People
Ofcom	Office of Communications
Opportunity Age	A consultation paper published by the Department for Work and Pensions in March 2005, Cm 6466
Wanless Report	Final Report of the Review by Derek Wanless, *Securing our Future Health: Taking a Long-Term View*, April 2002

Acronyms

AARP	American Association of Retired Persons
AT	Assistive technology
BBSRC	Biotechnology and Biological Sciences Research Council
BGS	British Geriatrics Society
BME	Black and minority ethnic
BSG	British Society of Gerontology
BSRA	British Society for Research on Ageing
CFAS	Cognitive Functions and Ageing Study
CHD	Coronary heart disease
CSA	Chief Scientific Adviser
CT (scan)	Computerised axial tomography
DA(OP)	Ministerial Sub-Committee on Older People (a sub-committee of the Cabinet Domestic Affairs Committee)
DCMS	Department for Culture, Media and Sport
Defra	Department for Environment, Food and Rural Affairs
DfES	Department for Education and Skills
DfT	Department for Transport
DHHS	(United States) Department for Health and Human Services
DLB	Dementia with Lewy Bodies
DNA	Deoxyribonucleic acid
DoH	Department of Health

DVLA	Driver and Vehicle Licensing Authority
DTI	Department of Trade and Industry
DWP	Department for Work and Pensions
ECG	Electrocardiogram
ELSA	English Longitudinal Study of Ageing
EPIC	European Prospective Investigation of Cancer. EPIC-Norfolk is the part of this study based at Cambridge University.
EPSRC	Engineering and Physical Sciences Research Council
EQUAL	Extending the Quality of Life, an EPSRC initiative
ERA	Experimental Research on Ageing, a BBSRC initiative
ESRC	Economic and Social Research Council
EU	European Union (the Union of the three original European Communities, set up by the Maastricht Treaty, 1992)
FFRAOP	Funders' Forum for Research on Ageing and Older People
FP	Framework Programme for Research (of the European Union).
GHS	British General Household Survey
HLE	Healthy life expectancy
HSQ	Health Statistics Quarterly, published by the Office for National Statistics
HTA	Health Technology Assessment Programme (of the Department of Health)
ICT	Information and communication technology
LE	Life expectancy
LLSI	Limiting long-standing illness
MEC	Minority Elderly Care, a research project supported initiated by PRIAE and supported by the European Commission
MISC 29	A Cabinet committee, dissolved after May 2005, with the terms of reference "To oversee and drive forward policy on the ageing society"
MRC	Medical Research Council
MRI	Magnetic resonance imaging
NCAR	National Collaboration on Ageing Research
NCRI	National Cancer Research Institute
NDA	New Dynamics of Ageing Programme
NHS	National Health Service
NIA	(United States) National Institute on Aging
NICE	National Institute for Health and Clinical Excellence
NIH	(United States) National Institutes of Health

NSF	National Service Framework
ODPM	Office of the Deputy Prime Minister
OECD	Organisation for Economic Co-operation and Development
ONS	Office for National Statistics
OST	Office of Science and Technology
PRIAE	Policy Research Institute on Ageing and Ethnicity
PRP	Policy Research Programme (of the Department of Health)
RAE	Research Assessment Exercise
RCUK	Research Councils UK, a partnership of the seven UK research councils
ROS	Reactive oxygen species
SAGE	Science of Ageing, a BBSRC initiative
SEU	Social Exclusion Unit (of the Office of the Deputy Prime Minister)
SHARE	Survey of Health and Retirement in Europe
USO	Universal Service Obligation
WHO	World Health Organization
XCAR	Cross-Council Coordinating Committee on Ageing Research

Printed in the United Kingdom by The Stationery Office Limited
7/2005   312283   19585

ISBN 0-10-400730-3

9 780104 007303